Business Persons'

Guide to

Taxation in the 90's

A15043 049505

BY

HARRY GORDON OLIVER

CERTIFIED PUBLIC ACCOUNTANT

ATTORNEY AT LAW

ANTONINI PROFESSIONAL CORPORATION

EL DORADO
P R E S S

Distributed to the trade by: Slawson Communications, Inc. 1-800-SLAWSON

Library of Congress Cataloging-in-Publication Data
Oliver, Harry Gordon, 1944-
    Business Persons' Guide to Taxation in the 90's

The Author has attempted to ensure that all information in this book is accurate. However, errors can occur, rules and regulations regarding tax and other matters do vary from location to location and are changed from time to time. Therefore, the author and publisher disclaim responsibility for the complete accuracy of the text. And as is always mere common sense, the reader is cautioned to consult a qualified accountant or attorney regarding accounting or legal problems.

Publisher: Milton H. Johnson, Jr.
Managing Editor: Jack Howell
Designer: Kathleen M. Gadway
Developmental Editor: Jerrold Dickson

ISBN 0-9622569-1-9

Foreword

"Anyone can make money, but it takes a wise person to keep it."

—Fable

The Antonini Professional Corporation has advised thousands of clients over the years from all walks of life. Many have come to us with an idea for a business venture. Some have started a business, but were unsure about what form to use. Should they do it themselves, have a partner or use some type of corporation? Each situation is unique. There is no pat answer, but there is a way to best determine what is right for you. The goal of this book is to give you the tools to work with, basic advice to build upon and the general format to enable you to select the best form of doing business. The time spent planning what you want to do will pay dividends from the outset.

Additionally, the book gives you the basic rules of taxation. The book will not be outdated or obsolete in one year because the basic tax structure will probably remain the same at least until science discovers the 5th dimension. Of course, specifics such as, depreciation will continuously change. Remember, as long as we are civilized we will have to pay taxes because, as President F.D.R. said in 1936, "taxes, after all, are the dues that we pay for the privileges of membership in an organized society".

Too many people dash out and "go into business" only to fail within a year or two. This book will give you the tools, guidelines and sound advice that will enable you to "think it through" before you start. It highlights the do's and don't's of starting a business. This book will also help those who are already in business to better understand the complexities of nurturing the profitable growth of their enterprise.

Successful business people seek advice from professionals. That is why there are CPAs, lawyers and bankers to help you. This book focuses on the fundamental questions you need to address before dealing with these people. This will save you money in terms of reduced professional fees. When you go to a restaurant and the waiter asks what you want for dinner, you don't say "Bring me something." If you did, in all likelihood he would bring you the most expensive item on the menu. The same line of thinking should apply when dealing with your accountant, lawyers or the tax authorities. You need to prepare before your meetings with them. It will save you money, time, and in the final analysis give you a focused picture of what you need to be successful.

Harry Gordon Oliver II

Antonini Professional Corporation
1700 Montgomery Street,
Suite 225
San Francisco, CA 94111
(415) 433-1700
FAX (415) 788-1820

TABLE OF CONTENTS

Section One
Alternative Forms of
Business Ownership

_____

Getting Started:
Planning, Questions & Decisions

One of the most important aspects of a successful business is properly planning for the business. Luck quite often plays an important role, but unfortunately, as mere mortals, we have no control over luck. Planning starts when you contemplate a decision to enter into a business, and it never ends. Also, when you run your own business, it is not a 9 to 5 job; it's more like a 5 to 9 job (5 in the morning to 9 at night — 8, maybe even 9, days a week).

In deciding to start a business, the first analysis is of your own energy, drive and capability. Running your own business is going to take a lot of time, energy, drive and emotion. You may have to sacrifice those favorite weekend sporting events and outings with the family.

Caution

The next step is to prepare a business plan. It should start with a plan summary. The business plan summary should highlight the key aspects of the business, including:

- The objectives of the business.

- The products or services and the marketing plan for selling those goods and services.

- The management of the business.

- Acquiring the goods or service.

- Projections of the business income and expense over periods of time.

It is advantageous to have a written business plan that can be read by individuals such as your advisors, "partners," bankers, friends, etc. The written plan should also help you focus on whether you really mean what you say and whether there is any potential for the business. If you are not regimented enough to have a "full blown" business plan, you certainly need to jot down as many pros and cons of the business opportunity as you can think of. The business plan should help you focus on potential problems or opportunities. It should also serve as a focal point or yardstick by which you can measure your actual results (financial and otherwise) with your intentions.

The goals and business intentions element of the business plan should help you fine tune what you want to do. It would be disastrous to not initially limit what you want to do so you can focus on achievable goals and business objectives. After you are successful, you can expand the business goals, products, etc.

The market analysis segment of the plan will help you focus on whether there is a market for your particular goods or services or some of your intended goods or services. In the market analysis you should determine whether there is a need for your business goods or services and who the competition, if any, is. You should also focus on how you will deliver the goods and services to the market. This part of the plan will help you analyze your market —

the geographical area, a price range for your goods or services, etc. The market analysis and how to deliver the goods or services is a very important aspect of a business. The best product in the world will be a "bust" if there is no plan to deliver it to buyers. In preparing the plan, be honest with yourself and realistic.

A business plan should cover the operations of the business. Where will it be located? What will be the source of employees for the business, transportation, etc.? The management of the organization needs to be planned. Will you initially do it yourself or will you need management for some aspects of the business while you concentrate on sales, etc.?

A very important element of the plan is the financial projections for the business. It will help you focus on the funds you need for the business, the volume of the business you need in order to break even, and the enormous expenses you may incur in order to make the business successful. The projections should be made and then critically reviewed and changed. The goal is to be as objective as you can so you will know what you are getting into. You should determine whether the revenue that you project is feasible or a "daydream." Again, be honest with yourself. Don't let your daydreams or ego get in the way of realistic analysis. You should consider all the expenses that you may incur. Don't forget to look at all those miscellaneous expenses that will all too often pop up. Such miscellaneous expenses may include health insurance for employees, transportation, janitors, insurance, etc., etc., etc. You may need to review financial statements from similar businesses for an analysis of all the possible expenses. Libraries, banks, etc., have materials that indicate the various expenses and the ratios of such expenses to revenue, etc., for your business.

The projections should be for a short term, such as one month, and then quarterly, annually, etc. This will provide you with a yardstick to use as you proceed. Initially, long term projections should be made to determine where you will be in two years, five years, etc. That may help you determine whether your business opportunity is going to be worth it. If all that energy results in a break-even operation after five years, it may not be worth it. You may decide to be a nonowner employee, free to watch sports on weekends.

When you have developed your business plan and fine tuned it (hopefully, several times), ask someone to look at it critically (but graciously if you are sensitive) and make adjustments based on feedback. Your family, friends, banker, business associates, etc., may be kind enough to review your plan and comment on it. In the plan you should attempt to think of everything that can go wrong and defend against it. For example, if your business will consist of offering weekend training sessions to men desiring to enhance their abilities, you should make sure your biggest event of the year is not planned for Super Bowl Sunday. The best planned event on the wrong day may result in disaster for a business that would otherwise be successful because of the demand for the goods or services offered by the business. The point is, take time and energy to think of everything.

There are many sources of information on business plans. The SBA publishes short, 3 or 4 page management aids to help in preparing a business plan and more thorough information such as booklets on business plans, etc. (See Appendix I and II.) Also, there are many books, articles, etc., on the subject.

The business plan should be revised annually. The revision should correct ideas, etc., in the initial plan that simply will not work out and allow the business to change as it becomes successful and grows, new trends develop, etc. Finally, the business plan should not be a document that is prepared and then lost or forgotten. It can serve as a reminder and a focal point as business continues. The business plan should be there to help you.

Starting a business without a plan — written, well reasoned and honest — will clearly result in disaster unless it turns out that you are one of the luckiest people in the world.   **Caution**

What are the frequently encountered problems for small business?

A major problem is simply inadequate planning. Preparing a business plan and critically and honestly reviewing it should go a long way in preventing this problem. Once the business plan is developed, you have to execute it — do what you said you would do in the plan.

Failure to adequately capitalize or have a secondary source of capital is often a problem. The business plan will again help with such problems in that it should point out the capital needed for a particular goal. This may result in changing the goals or looking for more capital at the beginning of the business. If additional capital is needed and the business has an honest potential, additional sources of funds may be from home equity or even the "in-laws" (but if the business ultimately fails, it could result in you being an "outlaw").

The inability to respond quickly to changing markets, demands, trends, costs of producing your goods and services, etc., can be a serious problem. The ability to quickly and efficiently respond to such changes may be helpful in keeping you in business or sending you to "the head of the class."

Similarly, the inability to deal with success by making necessary adjustments can be a problem. As the business becomes successful, the business owner will have to delegate more responsibility. This may be quite difficult for some people. Also, the business may have to expand its facilities, locations, employees. etc. You do not want to lose a good customer or client because he has decided to order more goods or services from you and you do not respond by adequately enhancing your ability to provide such goods and services.

Many businesses fold because they simply do not have the accounting and bookkeeping capability required to know where they are financially. A proper and adequate system of books and records is a must. You may think you are doing great because sales are substantial and increase every day. However, if you do not have the books and records that indicate that the cost of securing those sales are far in excess of the sales, you are going to ultimately find out the hard way. Do not be penny wise and pound foolish when it comes to keeping the books and records. You may have to hire an accountant in-house to keep the books and records, or you may have to provide accounting data to a CPA firm to provide you with monthly and/or quarterly financial statements and information as needed for your business.

As indicated above, it is quite important that the small business owner realizes the time and energy commitment that will be required of him as the business is started and grows. Once the business is successful, it is a requirement that you delegate responsibilities — although even then there will be a substantial time commitment required as you oversee the operations of the business.

Caution

Problems frequently encountered in the operation of a small business are:

- Failure to adequately plan for the business.

- Failure to quickly change due to changing markets, costs of providing goods and services.

- Inability to make the necessary changes required as business grows, etc.

- Failure to maintain adequate books and records.

In summary, when deciding whether to go into a particular business and once the business is up and running, key elements to success include planning, planning, planning, and revising the plan. Energy and a time commitment are absolutely necessary. Accounting for the results of operations is an absolute must and will provide information that will allow you to change your business plan, operations, etc., in order to be successful.

An alternative to starting a new business is buying an existing business or entering a business as a franchisee. The advantage of buying an existing business is that you already know there is a demand for the goods or services offered by the business. That may save time, the emotional drain of starting your own business, etc. A disadvantage of buying an existing business is that you may have to pay more for the existing business than you would have paid in starting your own business. You may also buy a business that has "peaked" and may start a decline due to market forces, lack of goodwill of the business, etc.

Franchising is essentially a plan of distribution under which an individually owned business is operated as part of a larger chain. A most obvious example of a successful franchise is McDonalds. The advantages of starting a business as a franchisee are that the business plan is provided for you and you need little experience, a relatively small amount of capital and you should have a well developed image. Centralized training and advertising are also a benefit. The disadvantages are the standardized method of operations that will be required of the franchisee and the inability to act as an entrepreneur and profit therefrom. Initially, substantial amounts are paid to the franchiser.

An individual can "start his own business" by buying an existing business or by entering business as a franchisee. There are pros and cons, benefits and burdens of each alternative.

Points to Remember

CHAPTER

TWO

_____

General Business

Considerations

Form of Business

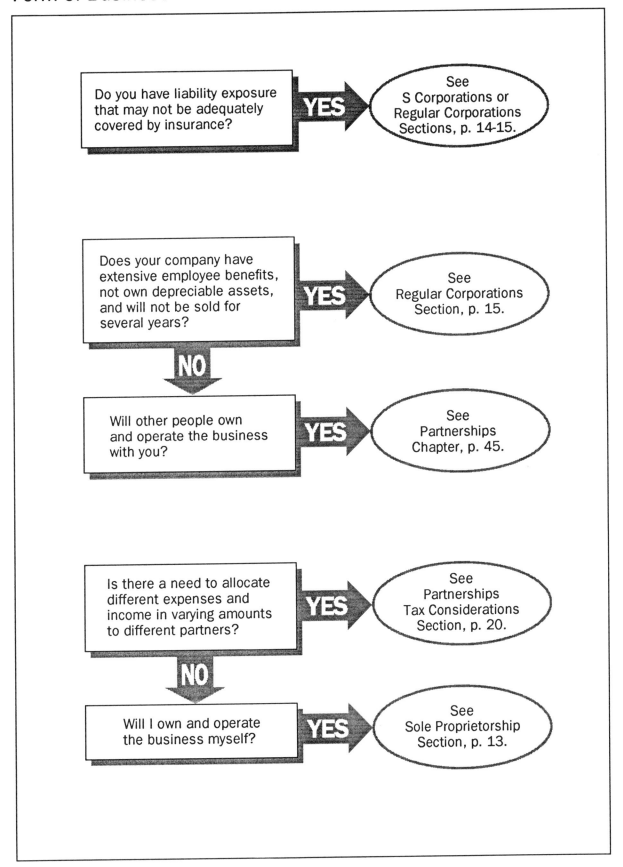

Do you have liability exposure that may not be adequately covered by insurance? — **YES** → See S Corporations or Regular Corporations Sections, p. 14-15.

Does your company have extensive employee benefits, not own depreciable assets, and will not be sold for several years? — **YES** → See Regular Corporations Section, p. 15.

NO ↓

Will other people own and operate the business with you? — **YES** → See Partnerships Chapter, p. 45.

Is there a need to allocate different expenses and income in varying amounts to different partners? — **YES** → See Partnerships Tax Considerations Section, p. 20.

NO ↓

Will I own and operate the business myself? — **YES** → See Sole Proprietorship Section, p. 13.

The first question you face once you've done your homework and decided to go into business is "What legal form should I use for my business?" For the vast majority of cases, your choices are to conduct the business as a sole proprietor, in the form of a partnership, or as a corporation. Business also can be conducted as a trust; however, since this form is very rare, we will not cover that alternative. Below we discuss some important considerations for each of the more commonly used business structures.

A sole proprietor is taxed on all income earned, less the deductible expenses incurred each year in the business. As a sole proprietor, an individual is subject to various liabilities resulting from the operation of the business. Examples of such liabilities include monetary damages for negligence or wrongful actions, such as breach of contract. In this litigious society of ours, an important consideration for the sole proprietor is the potential liability from an accident that may result in injury or property damage to another party. This is commonly referred to as "tort" liability.

If someone slips and falls in your place of business and suffers a serious injury, you may be liable for substantial medical expenses as well as an assessment for "pain and suffering." When you are a sole proprietor, your potential liability is not limited to your business assets, but extends to your personal assets as well.

You are conducting business as a sole proprietor. One day you accidentally run over a pedestrian while delivering goods to a customer. The pedestrian may sue to recover damages for his/her injury. The amount that pedestrian may collect is not limited to your business assets. If those business assets are not sufficient to satisfy a legal judgment against you, the pedestrian may also recover from your personal assets such as your car, home, jewelry, or other investments.

Having proper liability insurance is one way to protect a sole proprietor from various liabilities. However, there are limits to insurance coverage, including price (there is a limit to how much it makes sense for you to pay in premiums), types of risks covered (intentional acts typically are not covered), and policy limits. If you have $100,000 coverage but the damage costs come to $250,000, the claimant can go after your assets.

The limited liability resulting from doing business as a corporation is an important consideration for many individuals when deciding what form their business should be. If a business is properly incorporated and the various corporate formalities are adhered to (e.g., proper recordkeeping, filing of appropriate forms with government authorities, etc.), liability incurred in the course of conducting business (breach of contract and tort liability for injuries, etc.) will be limited to the assets of the corporation. In other words, the corporate "shell" provides protection of your personal assets from tort or other liabilities of the corporation.

What Form is Best for My Business?

Working as a Sole Proprietor

Example

In the example above, the pedestrian injured in the course of a business operation could recover only from assets owned by the corporation and could not procure the personal assets such as the family residence of the corporate shareholder.

Caution

Failure to follow the strict legal corporate formalities required by law may leave you open to personal liability. In some cases, injured parties have been able to "pierce the corporate shell" to reach the personal assets of corporate owners.

Do not think, however, that incorporating a business will limit in all situations the business owner's liability. A business owner cannot rid himself of liability by forming an undercapitalized corporation. An undercapitalized corporation might exist when the potential for injury, etc., is substantial. For example, an individual in the demolition business, knowing that the potential for injury or harm to people or property is substantial, may not avoid personal liability by incorporating with little or no capital. Limited liability may not be attained by an owner as a result of negligent conduct as a corporate employee or outrageous acts as a director. For example, a director's decision to operate without liability insurance when the business is substantially dangerous to employees, bystanders, the community, etc. may result in the director having personal liability for the decision. Finally, personal liability cannot be avoided by incorporating with a fraudulent intent to limit liability.

Caution

Incorporating is not a guaranteed way for the business owner to limit his or her liability. A shareholder may be liable if the corporation is undercapitalized, he/she is negligent as an employee or director, or if the corporation is formed with a fraudulent intent of limiting liability.

S Corporation

By electing to have the corporate business "taxed" as an S Corporation, an individual may secure the benefit of limited liability by incorporating and still be treated as the owner of the business for tax purposes. S Corporation status is only a tax characterization. Income passes through the S Corporation to its owner(s) who are then taxed at their personal rates. However, an S Corporation is still a separate legal entity. Properly maintained, it provides the owners with protection from liability resulting from corporate activities.

Partnership

If more than one individual owns the trade or business, they may choose to conduct the business in partnership form. However, as in a sole proprietorship, each general partner is fully responsible for all the liabilities of the partnership. In this respect, the partnership is more like the sole proprietorship than the corporate form of conducting business.

The liability problem for some of the partners may be resolved by forming a limited partnership. Limited partners typically will not be involved in the operation of the business although they can have a limited role. Usually they only provide capital for the business while the general partner(s) run the day-to-day operations. Limited partners are more like passive investors than partners. General

Fringe Benefits	Proprietor or Partnership	Corporation
Health Insurance	Premiums for proprietor/ partner only partly deductible during 1989, 1990.	Premiums deductible by corp.: not income to shareholder.
Group Term Life Insurance	Premiums for proprietor/ partner not deductible: paid with after-tax funds.	Premiums deductible by corp.: not income to shareholder.
Disability Insurance (Both Group & Personal)	Premiums for proprietor/ partner not deductible: paid with after-tax funds.	Premiums deductible by corp.: not income to shareholder. If paid by corp., the proceeds will be taxable.
Payment of Uninsured Medical Expenses	Premiums for proprietor/ partner not deductible: paid with after-tax funds.	If nondiscriminatory plan exists, may be paid by corp., excluded by employee.

Table 2.1

partners agree contractually to absorb the liability exposure for their limited partners.

In addition to the liability issue, businesses historically have been conducted in the corporate form because of the numerous tax advantages in the area of pension and profit sharing plans. However, federal tax law changes effected in 1982 eliminated most of those advantages. [1]

Regular Corporation

There are still advantages to conducting business in corporate form. One of the major beneficial areas concerns fringe benefits; Table 2.1 details the advantages of the corporate form business.

There are rules to insure that many of the above-mentioned benefits are not provided to employees in a manner that will discriminate in favor of an employee/owner. If such benefits are offered in a discriminatory manner, they may be included in the recipient's income. In 1986 Congress passed complicated rules to prevent almost any discrimination in favor of owner/employees. After small business voiced objections the legislation was appealed. In addition, the corporate form provides the opportunity to defer compensation if the corporation has an accounting period that ends on some date other than December 31. This allows the corporation to defer compensating the shareholder/employee from one year to the next year, which may be advantageous in some tax situations. (See Chapter Seven for a full discussion of deferred compensation rules.)

---

[1] The major advantage for corporations was that a greater amount of profits could be contributed to a pension or profit sharing plan benefitting the owners and deducted from taxable income than if the business were conducted in some other form. In 1982 general conformity was enacted for federal tax purposes between contributions and benefits available for corporations and other types of business forms.

Example

An employee of X Corporation may defer taxation of a bonus from the corporation from 1989 to 1990. If the corporation's tax year ends in February, the individual may declare and receive the bonus in February 1990 rather than December 1989. The corporation will then be entitled to a deduction for employee payments in its 1990 tax year.

The employee has deferred taxation one year. There will of course be withholding taxes on the bonus. However, such withholding taxes may be less than the employee's ultimate tax liability. For example, Federal withholding on a bonus is 20% but the employee may be in a 33% tax bracket without many withholding allowances or exemptions. When the employee's tax for 1990 is due (usually April 15, 1991), the additional amount will have to be paid then. Remember though, that the employee will have had the use of the tax savings for an extended time. If the money was invested intelligently, there could be a net benefit.

Individuals may deduct as ordinary loss up to $100,000 from the sale, exchange or worthlessness of small business stock. Losses in excess of $100,000 are deductible as capital losses. Small business stock is stock of a domestic corporation issued by a corporation to a partnership or individual, if the amount of money and adjusted basis of other property contributed to the corporation as capital does not exceed $1 million. Additionally, the corporation issuing the small business stock cannot have a substantial amount of passive income such as interest, dividends and royalties.

Example

Fygone One Corporation was formed in 1990 by a contribution of $500,000 in cash by Alpha and property having a fair market value of $1 million by Bravo. The adjusted basis of the assets contributed by Bravo was $500,000. Alpha received one-third of the stock issued and Bravo received two-thirds. The next year, due to competition and a general decrease in demand for Fygone One's products, the company ceased business operations and its stock became worthless. Alpha and Bravo are each entitled to an ordinary loss of $100,000 with the balance of the losses incurred by Alpha and Bravo being deductible as capital losses.

Being able to partly treat the losses as ordinary losses is a tax advantage to shareholders of small business corporations because ordinary losses can be deducted against any income. Capital losses can only be deducted against capital gains and $3,000 of ordinary income. Ordinary loss treatment is only available for stock issued by the corporation to the shareholder. It does not apply when a shareholder buys stock from another shareholder, subsequent to the formation of, or contribution to, the corporation.

Important

Professional corporations, such as those offering medical, legal, architectural, or accounting services, are usually required to use a tax year ending on December 31. If these corporations wish to deduct salary or bonus payments made during the year, those payments must be made by December 31.

Two recent changes in the tax laws have diminished the advantages of doing business as a corporation. First, individual tax rates have declined relative to corporate tax rates; and second, if a corporation sells its assets and liquidates, or simply liquidates, there is now a double tax—a tax at the corporate level and the shareholder level.

In 1990 and subsequent years, the federal tax rates for individuals generally will be lower than the rates for corporations. (Of course, tax laws constantly change. There is no assurance this current relationship will exist indefinitely.) In 1988 and subsequent years the maximum federal individual tax rate is 28% (because of "simplification," in certain situations the tax rate will be 33% due to the phase out of certain benefits), whereas the corporate maximum marginal tax rate is generally 34%.

The California maximum tax rate for both individuals and corporations is 9.3%. Previously the California individual rate was higher than the corporate rate. New York's rate in 1990 is 7.375% (7% after 1990) for individuals and 9% for corporations.

Federal corporate tax rules and some states, such as California, New York and other states that generally conform to federal rules, impose a double tax on the liquidation of a corporation. If a corporation's assets are sold and the proceeds are distributed to shareholder(s), or if the assets are simply distributed to shareholder(s), the corporation will pay a tax on the difference between the tax basis of the assets sold or distributed and their fair market value. This recent development is a substantial change from the previous California, New York and federal tax rules pertaining to corporate liquidations. Previously, a corporation could sell its assets, distribute the sales proceeds, and liquidate without incurring a corporate tax on the sale of the assets.

Recent Changes Diminish Appeal of Corporations

Assume you conduct a corporate-form real estate business consisting of the rental of one office building. If your corporation sells the building and distributes the sales proceeds to the individual shareholders, the shareholders would, of course, recognize gain. They would pay tax on the difference between the shareholders' basis in their stock and the fair market Value of the cash received from the corporation. But now, in accordance with relatively recent tax law changes, the corporation will also have to pay a tax on the gain from the sale of the real property before distribution to its shareholders. The corporation would distribute the cash proceeds, less the tax paid by the corporation. Previously, there would have been no tax at the corporate level.

Example

Because of the double taxation on the proceeds of a liquidated corporation, it may be advantageous for many more companies to conduct business in noncorporate form or as an S Corporation because S Corporations generally are not subject to the double tax. (See Chapter Two for details on S Corporations.)

Tax Tip

1   Business owners should conduct their business in corporate form if their business is one that has a potential for liability.

Points to Remember

2   Tax considerations may favor conducting business in noncorporate form or as an S Corporation, where taxes are assessed at the individual's level rather than at the corporate level.

3   There may be some benefit derived from regular corporation status rather than S corporation status if the corporation:

- does not make substantial profits,
- has employee benefits,
- does not have depreciable assets, and
- has owners who do not plan to sell the business for several years.

Tax Considerations in Forming a Partnership or Corporation

Usually income or losses are not recognized when assets (business equipment, desks, chairs, etc.) are contributed to a partnership or corporation. However, if assets are contributed to a partnership or corporation with liabilities in excess of the basis of such assets, gain could be recognized in certain situations. Also, if the corporation assumes certain debt, the person from whom the debt is assumed may have to recognize income.

Example

If you contribute an office building with a large outstanding mortgage balance to a newly formed corporation, your "basis" (purchase price adjusted by things such as any depreciation you may have taken in previous years), relative to the mortgage balance, will determine whether you have a taxable event.

Caution

The transfer or contribution of assets to a corporation are tax free **only** if the person transferring the property receives only stock and is in **control** of the corporation immediately after the transfer. Control generally means that the transferring person or persons own 80% or more of the stock of the corporation. Generally, before October 3, 1989 income (which, of course, is taxable to the individual) is also recognized to the transferring person if the individual receives, in exchange, assets from the corporation other than "securities" (e.g., shares of stock in the company). After October 2, 1989 income may be recognized if the taxpayers forming the corporation receive anything other than stock. In other words, income may be recognized to the extent debt is received if appreciated property is transferred to the corporation.

Example

If you transfer a computer to your corporation, before October 3, 1989 you may be liable for taxes if (1) you receive a note from the corporation in exchange for the computer AND (2) the note is to be paid off by the corporation within two or three years. After October 2, 1989 income is recognized if anything other than stock is received.

In forming a corporation, it may be advisable to receive a note (that is paid off over at least a five year period) as well as stock of the corporation. Generally, the debt to equity ratio should not be greater than 4 to 1. And, as indicated above, debt should not be received if appreciated property is contributed to the corporation.

The advantage of the business owner receiving debt as well as stock from the formation of the corporation is that interest on the debt is deductible by the corporation and the repayment of the debt does not result in income to the shareholder/creditor.

Example

Glenco was formed in January 1990 by a contribution of $500,000 by Big Bucks, a wealthy individual businessman. Based on advise from his accountant and attorney, the corporation issued stock for $100,000 of the contribution and debt for $400,000. The debt was to be paid off over a five year period and paid interest at the market rate for such debt. Interest payable on the debt is deductible by the corporation and includable in Big Bucks' income. The repayment of principal on the debt is neither deductible by the corporation nor included in the income of Big Bucks.

Issuing debt as well as stock may be advantageous to business owners in certain situations. In the above example, if Big Bucks does not participate in the business, he may not be entitled to "strip out" cash from the corporation as deductible compensation. If the payments to him are treated as dividends, there will be double taxation — once at the corporate level on the corporate profits and once at the shareholder level on the dividends. The repayment of debt avoids tax at the shareholder level. The corporation will have to pay tax on the income used to repay the debt, however.

A downside of issuing debt as well as stock is that any ultimate worthlessness of the debt will generally be treated as a capital loss rather than an ordinary loss that may be available for small business stock, as discussed above. Because of the $100,000 limitation of ordinary losses on small business stock, capital loss treatment may not be avoided if substantial funds are contributed to a corporation.

In most cases a partnership must use a calendar year (January 1 to December 31) for tax purposes if the majority of its partners are individuals on a calendar year. Corporations, other than personal service corporations and S Corporations, may use any taxable year.

Example

A regular corporation may elect a June fiscal year end and benefit from the deferral attributable to paying bonuses between January and June, as set forth above.

Points to Remember

1   A corporation or partnership may be formed and assets contributed without recognizing income or loss.

2   To avoid taxation, a transferor must control (own 80% or more) of a corporation but need not control a partnership.

3   Income may be recognized in certain situations if debt is transferred to a partnership or corporation.

Tax Considerations in Operating a Partnership

There is a substantial difference in the tax treatment of partnerships and regular corporations. Income and losses of a partnership flow through to the individual partners and are treated as the income or expenses of the partner. Thus, the individual partners pay tax on the income rather than the partnership. There is **never** any double taxation, because a partnership itself never pays income tax.

In most cases a partner does not recognize income or loss on the termination of the partnership and distribution or return of the partnership's assets to the partners. A partnership then avoids the double taxation upon liquidation that corporations face.

Another benefit of being a partnership, rather than a regular corporation or an S Corporation, is the ability to specially allocate the income or losses of the partnership in ratios which may not correspond to how the partners actually own the partnership. (See Chapter Four for details on Partnerships.)

Example

If A and B are each 50/50 partners in a partnership, for good business reasons, the income or loss may be allocated 75% to A and 25% to B, or in some other fashion. This can only be done in the regular corporation or S Corporation form of conducting business by paying salaries **before** the year end, which may be difficult.

Many individuals may be conducting business as a partnership but are unaware of it.

Example

If you and a friend are co-owners of an apartment building and you provide services to your tenants, the ownership may be treated as a partnership rather than mere co-ownership.

The tax consequences are usually the same, but in some situations, specific elections must be made with respect to the tax treatment of certain transactions in order to preserve certain tax benefits of a partnership form. If such elections are not made by filing the proper forms with the tax authorities, it is possible to lose favorable tax treatment in certain transactions or situations. (See Chapter Four for details on Partnerships.)

Tax Tip

For profitable small businesses, it may be better to conduct the business as a partnership or as a corporation that elects to be taxed as an S Corporation (see discussion below).

Tax Considerations of Operating Corporations and S Corporations

Regular corporations, in contrast to partnerships, are subject to taxes on their income. Generally, the taxable income of closely held corporations (as opposed to large publicly owned companies) is reduced to minimal amounts by paying most of the income to the shareholder/employees as compensation for services rendered, rental of property, and other legitimate expenses. The corporation gets a deduction for paying expenses such as wages, rent, and interest. This deduction would include amounts paid to shareholder/employees.

One hitch is that if the compensation or other expenses are not "reasonable," the excess amount will not be deductible by the corporation. The tax authorities make their judgments of "reasonableness" based on a number of tests. These include determining if the compensation is more than what would be paid to an employee who is not a shareholder. The nondeductible compensation, rent, or other expenses would be treated as a dividend (a nondeductible expense for corporations) to the shareholder/employee. It would still be included in the individual's income. The corporation would then wind up paying additional income taxes since the dividend is not deductible, as salary would be.

Caution

The shareholders of a regular corporation recognize income when the corporation liquidates and distributes its assets. The gain will be the amount of the difference between the shareholders' basis (price paid for the stock) in the stock and the fair market value of the assets received. Additionally, the corporation would recognize income in the amount of the difference between the corporation's basis in the assets distributed and the fair market value of the assets.

The tax consequences of S Corporation operations are a little more complicated. Entities that elect to be treated as S Corporations when they incorporate are not subject to taxes. The income and, to some extent, the losses flow through to the shareholders much like a partnership. Entities that were regular corporations (a corporation that did not elect to be treated as an S Corporation from its beginning) before 1987 may be subject to taxation in certain situations. (See Chapter Three for details on S Corporations.)

Similar to regular corporations, an S Corporation must recognize income on the difference between the basis in its assets and the fair market value of such assets when it distributes the assets to its shareholders. The income recognized by the corporation flows through to the shareholders. Thus, only one tax is paid, a better resolution than when a regular corporation liquidates but not as desirable as the result when a partnership liquidates.

Points to Remember

1 The tax consequences attributable to the operation of a partnership, a regular corporation, and an S corporation vary.

2 Partnerships are much more flexible in reporting and allocating profits and losses, and never pay income taxes.

3 Corporations are often subject to income taxation.

   a Corporations will generally have to pay tax when appreciated assets are distributed to shareholders.
   b Partnerships will not pay tax in such situations.

4 S Corporation status usually avoids the double taxation that confronts regular corporations.

Federal/State Tax [Non]Conformity!

States that collect individual and corporate income taxes can have their own rules that are distinctly different from the federal rules, adopt in total the federal rules, or a combination of the two. Most states have the latter approach. States that use the federal rules entirely or even to some extent are said to have conformity or partial conformity.

California is an example of a state that has adopted what should be called partial conformity. Following is a list of California rules that are different than the federal rules.

■ California allows only 50% of a net operating loss to be carried forward. It does not allow any carryback of net operating losses.

■ There is conformity in the methods of computing depreciation for property placed in service on or after January 1, 1987, but only for individuals. There is no conformity for corporate purposes. California continues to use the facts and circumstances test for corporate depreciation. Also, there continues to be a substantial difference for both individual and corporate purposes when computing depreciation on property placed in service before January 1, 1987.

■ The California standard deduction is lower than the federal amount. It is $1,966 for a single person or a married person filing separately, and $3,932 for a married joint return couple.

■ California allows a credit against the tax rather than a deduction for personal exemptions. For 1988 the credit is $50 for a single person or a married person filing a separate return, $104 for a joint return, $50 for each additional dependent, and $52 for each person age 65 and over, or blind.

■ For years beginning on or after January 1, 1988, California taxes limited partnerships for the privilege of doing business in the State of California. The tax is $300 in 1988, $600 in 1989, and $800 in 1990 and subsequent periods.

■ California allows a credit equal to 4.5% of the capital gain on the sale of residential rental property if it was held for more than five years. The credit is 3% of the capital gain if the property was held for more than one year, but not more than five years.

■ California does not allow a credit for rehabilitation of historic structures.

■ California does not require payment of estimated taxes by estates and trusts.

■ Unemployment compensation is taxable in full for federal purposes. It is excluded in full for California purposes.

■ Social Security benefits are partially taxable for federal purposes but fully excluded for California purposes.

■ Winnings in the California state lottery are fully included in gross income for federal tax purposes. They are excluded from gross income for California tax purposes.

California now creates conformity by specifically adopting a prior federal tax act through an act of the state legislature. Certain items may be specifically excluded from conformity when California adopts a recently enacted federal act. The adoption of new federal rules generally must be done by March 15 of the year following the year for which the rules are to be effective. California has adopted many of the federal '87 and '88 changes and will probably adopt many of the '89 changes.

S Corporations

S Corporations

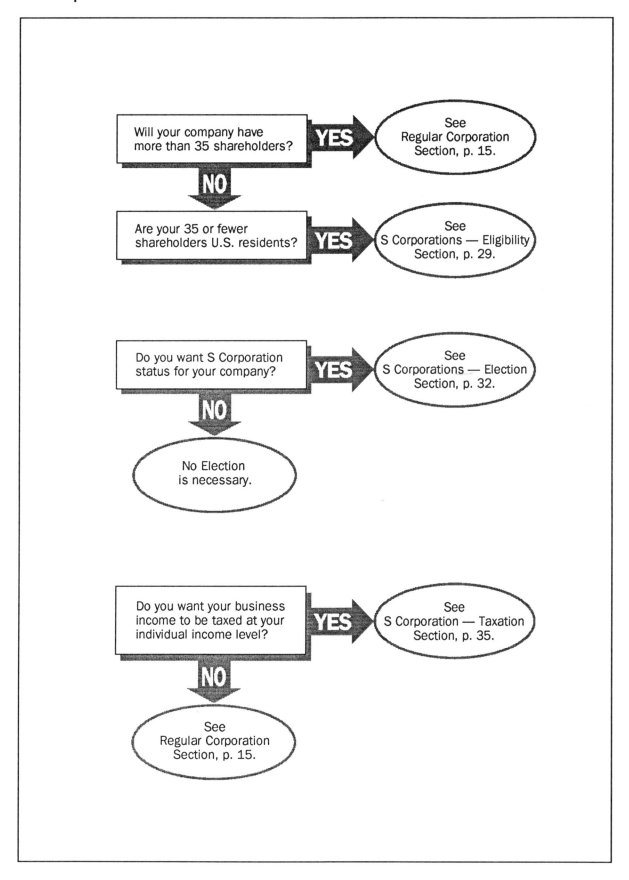

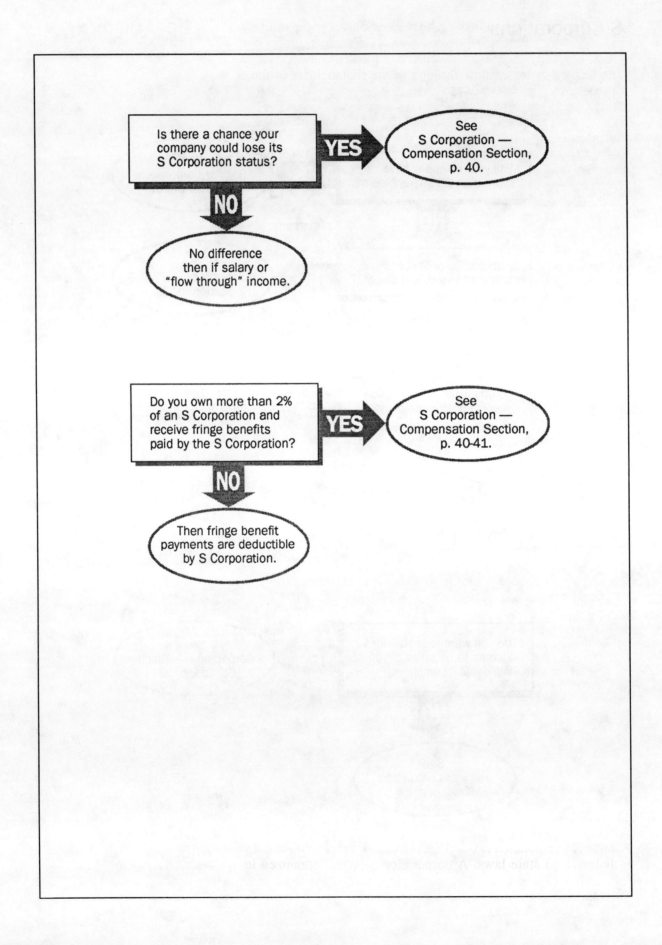

A Brief History of S Corporations

An S Corporation is an entity that is incorporated under state law and specifically elects to be treated as an S Corporation for tax purposes. Normally an S Corporation is not subject to income taxes. The income or losses flow through to the shareholders of the S Corporation. The shareholders then pay taxes on the income or deduct the losses on their individual tax returns.

Not all states that have a corporate and individual tax have S corporation rules. And the states that have such rules do not necessarily completely conform to the federal S corporation rules. Thirty-nine states recognize some form of S corporation status. (See Appendix III.)

Prior to 1987, California did not have the equivalent of the federal rules for S Corporations. In late 1987, California passed legislation to bring state tax laws into closer conformity with federal laws. That legislation created S Corporations for California tax purposes. The rules were effective retroactively to the beginning of 1987.

While further legislation in 1988 modified the California S Corporation rules to improve conformity to the federal rules, there are still substantive differences. The California variances from the federal rules are set forth in more detail on page 40.

As a result of changes occasioned by the 1986 Tax Reform Act, S Corporations are a preferred way of operating for many small businesses. In the following pages, we delineate the major advantages and disadvantages of this form of business operation.

Eligibility

Only certain corporations are eligible to be S Corporations under federal and many state rules. An entity must meet the following requirements to be considered an S Corporation:

1   An S Corporation must be a "domestic corporation."

2   Only individuals, estates or certain types of trusts may be S Corporation shareholders.

3   An S Corporation may not have a nonresident alien as a shareholder.

4   An S Corporation must not have more than 35 shareholders.

5   An S Corporation may not have more than one class of stock.

6   An S Corporation may not be an "ineligible corporation."

7   An entity may not elect to be an S Corporation if it lost S Corporation status within the four prior tax years.

Those requirements which are not self-explanatory are explained below.

What Is a Domestic Corporation?

A domestic corporation is one that is created or organized pursuant to federal and state laws. A corporation properly organized in California will be a domestic corporation that can elect to be an S Corporation if it meets all the other requirements.

Who or What Can Be Shareholders?

A U.S. citizen can be an S Corporation shareholder. A nonresident alien individual cannot be a S Corporation shareholder. If a nonresident alien becomes a shareholder of an S Corporation, the corporation will not qualify to be an S Corporation from the time the nonresident becomes a shareholder. A nonresident alien is an individual who is neither a citizen nor a resident of the United States.

An individual who is not a U.S. citizen will be considered a resident (rather than a nonresident) of the U.S. if he has legal immigration status, (i.e., a "green card") or if he/she spends 180 days in the United States in any year (using a weighted average of number of days spent in the United States during the current year and prior two years).

It is important that shareholders who want to elect S Corporation status for their business check to determine that shareholders (or potential shareholders) are either U.S. citizens or resident aliens.

The estate of a deceased S Corporation shareholder (even a bankrupt estate) can be an S Corporation shareholder.

Trusts generally may not be S Corporation shareholders. However, certain trusts meeting very specific requirements may be shareholders. If the corporation or its shareholders contemplating electing S Corporation status anticipate having a trust as a shareholder, tax advice should be secured from an attorney or a CPA competent in S Corporation taxation.

Caution

A corporation or partnership may not be an owner of an S Corporation. Beneficial or real ownership, rather than legal ownership, is the basis on which the tests are made.

Example

Ozzie is listed as the legal owner of S Corporation stock of Ozz Corporation. However, Ozzie is holding the stock for Harriet — the real owner. Since Harriet is the real owner, she must sign the election forms and report her share of the income or loss.

How Many Shareholders Can an S Corporation Have?

Since 1983 an S Corporation can have up to 35 shareholders. Prior to that, the permitted number of shareholders was only 10 before 1976, and then 25 until 1983. The 35 shareholder-limit test is made each moment of the year. This simply means that a corporation can have more than 35 shareholders during the year and be an S Corporation as long as there are not more than 35 shareholders at any one time. Persons owning stock as co-owners will each be treated as an owner for purposes of the 35 shareholder limit.

Important

A husband and wife and their estates will be treated as one shareholder for purposes of the 35 shareholder rule.

Example

Tom, Dick, and Harry own one share of S Corporation stock as joint tenants. They are treated as three shareholders rather than one. The S Corporation can have only 32 other qualified shareholders to retain its special tax status.

Ineligible corporations include those types of corporations which have special tax benefits, such as domestic international sales corporations (which receive special tax benefits for foreign sales). They may not be S Corporations.

Also, an entity will not qualify to be an S Corporation if it owns 80% or more of the voting stock of another corporation and 80% or more of the value of such a corporation.

A corporation can be an S Corporation if it owns 79% of the stock of a "subsidiary" and the sole shareholder of the S Corporation owns the remaining 21%. With creative planning, some "no-no's" become possible. However, it is critical that you get professional advice in such situations to ensure full compliance with the law.

An S Corporation may only have one class of stock, but differences in voting rights are not necessarily treated as different classes of stock. An S Corporation can have voting and nonvoting common stock. **However, each share of stock must have the exact same economic rights.**

There is a potential problem if a corporation issues both stock and debt. If the proper precautions are not taken, the debt may be considered a second class of stock by the tax authorities. This situation would terminate S Corporation status.

Certain debt will not be treated as a second class of stock. Such debt must:

1 Be in writing.

2 Have an unconditional promise to pay a certain amount on a certain date.

3 Have interest rates and payments that are not contingent on profits, cash flow, or other business considerations.

4 Not be convertible directly or indirectly into stock.

5 Be owed to a creditor who would be a permitted shareholder.

An S Corporation usually must use a calendar year. However, there are exceptions to this rule. A corporation with calendar-year shareholders may use a fiscal year ending in September, October, or November. Also, an S Corporation can make a tax deposit and have a fiscal year rather than a calendar year.

An S Corporation can have an other-than-calendar year if it has a specific business purpose for doing so. A business purpose will be deemed to exist if more than 25% of the entity's gross receipts are incurred in the last two months of the fiscal year for each of the three preceding 12-month periods.

What Is an Ineligible Corporation?

Tax Tip

What Type of Stock May an S Corporation Have?

Caution

What Is the Permitted Taxable Year?

New corporations and corporations that fail the 25% test must convince the IRS and Franchise Tax Board there is a business purpose for using other than a calendar year end. They must base their case on facts and circumstances rather than prior history.

When Must the Tests Be Met?

A corporation must meet the various tests to be an S Corporation, **both** on the date the S Corporation election is made and on the first day of the taxable year the election is effective.

Example

An S Corporation election was filed on December 15, 1990 for Successful Products Corporation, to be effective for the year beginning January 1, 1990. One shareholder who signed the election form did not become a U.S. resident until December 31, 1990. The S Corporation election was therefore invalid. This corporation will not qualify as an S Corporation because a nonresident alien (or any other shareholder who is not an eligible shareholder) cannot own stock in the S Corporation any time during the first year in which the election is to be effective or when the election is made, if the election is made prior to the beginning of such year.

Points to Remember

1 An S Corporation is an entity which has been properly incorporated in California or another state **and** elected to be treated as an S Corporation solely for income tax purposes.

2 An S election does not affect the legal operation of the corporation. It only provides rules as to what extent the corporation or its shareholders pay tax on the income.

3 Not all corporations can elect to be S Corporations. Eligibility tests must be met in order for a corporation to qualify to make an S Corporation election.

   a The tests must be met when the S Corporation election is made **and** at all times during the S Corporation's tax year.

4 Usually an S Corporation must have a calendar year as its tax year.

5 If an entity was previously an S Corporation, in general it may not elect to be an S Corporation again until the fifth taxable year after the year in which the S Corporation status was terminated or revoked.

S Corporation Election

An S Corporation election is made by filing Form 2553 by the 15th day of the third month of the year for which the election is effective. A federal election is effective for purposes of California law as well. All shareholders must sign Form 2553 consenting to the election. Both spouses must sign consenting to the election if the stock is, in reality, community property even though only one spouse is shown as the owner on the corporate books and records. A corporate official must sign the form stating that the corporation "elects" to be an S Corporation.

If an election is filed after the first day of the corporation's taxable year, individuals who were shareholders on any day during the taxable year before the election was made (but not on the day the election was made) must still sign the form consenting to the election.

> A shareholder who sold stock during the tax year but before the election was made must sign Form 2553 consenting to the election.

Example

Form 2553, signed by all consenting shareholders and the corporate officer for the corporation, must be filed at the Internal Revenue Service Center where the corporation files, or will file, its income tax return. Such "service center" is the one which serves the state where the corporation has its principal business office.

The S Corporation election must be filed on or before the 15th day of the third month of the tax year for which the S election is to be effective. For a calendar year, this is the 15th day of March. A late election for one year will generally be effective for the next year. An election may be filed before the selected tax year begins.

Important

> An election can be filed in December for the tax year beginning the following January. However, to qualify for the elected year, it must be filed by March 15 of that calendar year.

Example

It is very important that the election to be an S Corporation is filed on time. If it is not, the corporation will not qualify as an S Corporation until the subsequent year. A new corporation should not elect to be an S Corporation until it has obtained a certificate of incorporation. In addition, the corporation should not elect until it has **either** (1) shareholders, (2) assets, or (3) does business.

In order to prove timely filing of the election and consents, Form 2553 should be sent via certified mail with a return receipt requested. The corporation should also request that the IRS stamp and return an enclosed copy of the transmitted letter sent with the form.

Tax Tip

1   An S Corporation election is made by filing IRS Form 2553 by the 15th of the third month of the year for which the election is effective.

Points to Remember

2   A federal election is usually sufficient for state purposes. But some states may require that an election be filed with the state's tax authorities to be valid for state purposes.

3   ALL shareholders must sign Form 2553 consenting to the S Corporation election.

4 **BOTH** spouses must sign Form 2553 if the stock is community property, even though only one spouse is shown as the owner of record on the corporate books.

Termination of S Corporation Status

After a valid S Corporation election, S Corporation status continues until there is a terminating event. There are generally three causes of termination. The first two causes are relatively easy to understand. The first cause occurs if the corporation and persons owning a majority of the S Corporation stock revoke the corporation's S Corporation election. The second cause occurs if a corporation ceases to meet any of the S Corporation eligibility tests delineated above.

Example

S Corporation status would be terminated if a nonresident alien becomes a shareholder or if the corporation had more than 35 shareholders at any one time.

The third cause of termination is a little more complicated. It comes into play when a corporation has had profits from taxable years prior to when it was an S Corporation and has had a substantial amount of passive investment income, such as dividends, interest, etc., in three consecutive years. This latter case is covered in more detail below. If you think your company may fall into this category, you should consult with a professional promptly.

Passive Income in Excess of 25% of Gross Receipts

An S Corporation may be terminated if it has too much passive income for a three-year period. This rule does not apply if an entity has been an S Corporation from its inception. However, it does apply if S Corporation status was elected after the initial year of incorporation and the S Corporation still has undistributed earnings dating from the time when it was not an S Corporation.

S Corporation status termination under this rule occurs only if passive investment income exceeds 25% of gross receipts. The 25% limit must be exceeded for each of three consecutive taxable years. If so, the S Corporation election terminates at the end of the third consecutive year.

Caution

There is an income tax at the corporate level for an S Corporation in any year in which the passive investment income exceeds 25% of gross receipts.

For purposes of these two rules, passive investment income means royalties, some, but not all, rents, dividends, interest, and gains from the sale or exchange of stock or securities. Gross receipts generally include all items of income received by the corporation. **However, only the gain (not the total sales price) from the sale or exchange of stock or securities or other capital assets is counted as gross receipts.**

Voluntary Revocation of S Corporation Status

A revocation made on or before the 15th day of the third month of the taxable year (March 15 for calendar year S Corporations) can be effective for the entire taxable year (i.e., from the first day of the year). A revocation made after such date will be effective on the date stated in the revocation, as long as it is on or after the date the revocation is made. It can be effective at the beginning of the next taxable year.

If an entity ceases to be a qualified S Corporation (because it has a nonresident alien shareholder, two classes of stock, etc.), termination is effective on the date of the terminating event. Such termination is not retroactive.

When S Corporation status is terminated during the taxable year, two taxable years will be created. One will be a short taxable year for the S Corporation part of the year. The other will be a short taxable year for the part of the year the corporation is not an S Corporation. Fortunately for the accounting industry, a tax return must be filed for each short taxable year.

Important

Inadvertent Termination of S Corporation Status

As you may already suspect from the maze of regulations surrounding S Corporation status, failure to continue to qualify to be an S Corporation may be voluntary or inadvertent. However, in cases where termination is inadvertent, termination of S Corporation status may be ignored by the IRS if certain tests are met.

Various procedures must be followed to assure that the IRS will ignore the termination. The problem causing the termination must be corrected as soon as possible. The S Corporation should check with its tax advisor about disclosing the issue and asking the IRS to excuse the termination.

1   An S Corporation election may be terminated intentionally, by accident, or due to preexisting circumstances.

Points to Remember

2   An S Corporation that has had too much passive income (more than 25% of gross receipts) will lose its S status if the excess passive income continues for three consecutive years.

3   Accidental terminations will occur if the corporation no longer meets the various tests to be an S Corporation.

4   Accidental termination could have disastrous tax consequences to a corporation and its shareholders.

5   In certain cases, inadvertent terminations will be ignored by the IRS. When the termination is discovered by the corporation, it must correct the problem immediately.

Normally S Corporations do not pay taxes. Instead, the income, losses, and "separately stated" items flow through to the shareholders of the S Corporation. The shareholders then pay taxes based on

Taxation of Income or Losses

their income. However, S Corporations may have to pay income taxes in certain situations.

An S Corporation may be subject to three taxes. First, as we mentioned above, an S Corporation may be subject to income taxes if its passive income exceeds 25% of the business's gross receipts. Second, if a regular corporation claims an investment tax credit and in a subsequent year elects to be an S Corporation, the S Corporation may have to "recapture" the investment tax credit if the asset is disposed of within three to five years after the property was purchased.

And finally, an S Corporation which made its S Corporation election before January 1, 1987, may have to pay a tax on capital gains if the gain meets three criteria: (1) the net capital gain exceeds $25,000, (2) net capital gain exceeds 50% of the S Corporation's taxable income, **and** (3) the S Corporation's taxable income exceeds $25,000.

Important

The tax on capital gains does not apply if the S Corporation has been an S Corporation for each of its three immediately preceding taxable years. Also, an entity that has been an S Corporation from its beginning is not subject to this tax.

Corporations electing S Corporation status after December 31, 1986, are not subject to this capital gains tax. However, they may be subject to a "built-in gains tax" during the first ten years in which the S Corporation election is applicable. A built-in gain is a recognized gain from the sale of property that had appreciated at the time of the S Corporation election.

Example

If a regular corporation owns real estate with a tax basis of $10,000 but is worth $20,000 when the election is made, the new electing S Corporation has a $10,000 built-in gain. It could be subject to tax on such gain if the property is sold during the first ten years after the election is made. If the real estate is sold in the 11th year after the S Corporation election, the S Corporation would not pay tax on such gain.

As enacted, the net tax in this situation was the lesser of the tax on the built-in gain or the tax on the taxable income of the S Corporation computed as if it were not an S Corporation. If the S Corporation does not have taxable income (computed as if it were not an S Corporation) because of operating expenses including salary, rents, etc., paid to the shareholders, it would not be subject to the built-in gains tax. Congress recently modified this rule and although it keeps the taxable income limitation, the built-in-gain carries over and may produce a tax during the 10-year built-in-gain period.

Important

The built-in gains tax does not apply if an entity has been an S Corporation from the beginning. A small corporation which elects to be treated as an S Corporation for a taxable year before 1989 may not be subject to part of the built-in gains tax. A small corporation is one that has ten or fewer shareholders. The value of the corporation stock must not exceed $5 million. Partial relief from the built-in gains tax is available if the fair market value of the corporate stock exceeds $5 million but did not exceed $10 million.

1 S Corporations generally do not pay income taxes.

2 In certain situations an S Corporation may be subject to a tax for the recapture of an investment tax credit taken before the corporation elected S status.

3 Corporations electing S status before 1986 may be subject to a tax on capital gains in very limited situations.

4 Corporations electing S status after 1986 may be subject to a tax when the corporation sells or transfers assets which were appreciated at the time the S election was made.

5 A corporation that has elected to be an S Corporation from the beginning is not subject to any tax.

Points to Remember

Pass Through of Income, Losses, and Deductions

An S Corporation's income or losses pass through to the shareholder in the shareholder's taxable year in which the S Corporation year ends.

> If an S Corporation has a November fiscal year end, the income for the 12 months ending in November 1990 will be included in the 1990 individual income tax return of the shareholder (assuming the shareholder has a calendar year end). If the S Corporation has a calendar year, the 1990 income of the S Corporation would also be reported on the 1990 individual income tax return of the shareholder.

Example

All income, losses, or deductions flow through to the shareholders. If the S Corporation pays a tax on capital gains or in the few other situations detailed above, such amount will reduce the income that flows through to the shareholders.

> If your S Corporation earns $100,000 of income, that amount would normally flow through to the shareholders. However, if the S Corporation had to pay a capital gains tax of $30,000, you would only have to report the pass through of $70,000 of income from the S Corporation.

Example

A shareholder has basis in stock equal to the amount of cash or the adjusted basis of other property contributed to the S Corporation, plus amounts loaned to the S Corporation. Such basis in stock and debt is increased by gains that pass through the corporation and is reduced by losses and deductions flowing from the corporation. Cash distributions (and the fair market value of other property) decrease the adjusted basis the shareholder has in the S Corporation.

Caution

A shareholder can only deduct losses and deductions that flow through the S Corporation to the extent the shareholder has basis in the S Corporation stock. To the extent losses and deductions exceed the shareholder's basis in the stock, the unused losses and deductions can be carried forward by the shareholder. They can then be used when the shareholder acquires additional basis in the S Corporation stock.

"Separately—Stated Items"

Various types of income that flow through the S Corporation to the shareholder must be separately stated rather than treated as part of the net income from operations of the S Corporation. The items that must be separately stated are generally the items that are treated separately or uniquely on the tax return of the shareholder.

For example, tax-exempt income of the S Corporation is stated separately because it is not taxable to the shareholder. Charitable contributions flow through separately because they are subject to various limitations on the individual's income tax return. Capital gains/losses and investment interest income/expenses are stated separately as well.

Important

The type of income that flows through the S Corporation is determined at the S Corporation level. This simply means that whether gain is considered ordinary income or capital gain is determined at the S Corporation level.

Distributions

An S Corporation must recognize gain (to the extent that the fair market value of the asset distributed exceeds its tax basis) on almost any distribution of property to a shareholder. Understand that this is distinct from the flow through of income earned in the operation of the business.

If an S Corporation does not have any retained profits from pre-S Corporation years, a distribution of cash or property that has not appreciated is tax free to the shareholder unless it exceeds the shareholder's basis in his S Corporation stock. The fair market value of the asset distributed in excess of the adjusted basis of the stock results in gain to the shareholder.

Important

The basis of S Corporation stock is measured at the year end **after** income or losses flow through to the shareholder rather than on the date of the actual distribution.

If a corporation has retained profits from pre-S Corporation years, distributions of property will result in dividend income to the shareholder to the extent the fair market value of the assets distributed exceeds the basis the shareholder has in his/her stock. To the extent the distributions exceed the retained profits from pre-S Corporation years, the gain is treated as gain from the sale of an asset.

There is a distinct disadvantage for an S Corporation in earning tax-exempt income. This is because the ultimate distribution of the cash resulting from the tax-exempt income will be taxable to the individual shareholders. Had the shareholders earned the tax-exempt income through their personal investments rather than through an S Corporation, the tax-exempt income would not be taxable to the individual.

Tax Tip

Points to Remember

1   An S Corporation generally does not pay taxes.

2   An S Corporation's income or losses flow through to its shareholders. The shareholders report their share of the income or loss and pay tax or offset other income, depending on the S shareholder's individual tax circumstances.

3   Items of income and expense that have special treatment at the individual level are stated separately by the S Corporation.

4   Losses can only be deducted by a shareholder to the extent the shareholder has basis in the S Corporation's stock.

5   If an S Corporation distributes appreciated property, it must recognize gain in the amount of the excess fair market value of the distributed asset over the corporation's adjusted basis in such asset. The gain flows through to the shareholder as part of the S Corporation's income.

6   Usually distributions of cash that do not exceed a shareholder's basis in the S Corporation's stock are not taxable.

Repayment of Shareholder Debt

A shareholder's portion of the losses which flow through an S Corporation can be used by the shareholder up to the extent he/she has basis in the S Corporation stock or to the amount of loans he/she has made to the S Corporation. Losses first reduce a shareholder's basis in stock. They then reduce the basis in loans to the corporation.

Income first increases the shareholder's basis in loans to the S Corporation. It then increases the basis in S Corporation stock. If a loan is repaid before income flows through and increases the shareholder's basis in the loan to its face amount, the repayment will result in gain to the shareholder. If the corporation issues a note to reflect the debt owed to the shareholder, a capital gain will result from repayment. If there is no corporate note and the debt is an open account, the gain will be treated as ordinary income rather than capital gain.

An increase in a shareholder's basis in his debt resulting from the flow through of income generally occurs at year end rather than pro rata during the year. Therefore, optimum tax planning suggests that repayment of the debt should be made in a year subsequent to the year in which income increases the shareholder's basis in debt.

Tax Tip

Example

Loss Corp. had $200,000 in losses in prior years that were deducted on the sole shareholder's Form 1040. The losses reduced the shareholder's basis in stock from $100,000 to zero and debt from $100,000 to zero. The debt was repaid to the shareholder while the basis was zero. The shareholder has $100,000 in gain which will be ordinary or capital, depending on whether a note was used for the debt or if it was made on an open account.

Points to Remember

1 A loan to an S Corporation generates basis for deducting losses flowing through from an S Corporation.

2 If the S Corporation repays the loan before the basis in the loan is increased by income flowing through the corporation, gain will be **unnecessarily** recognized.

3 If a loan to an S Corporation is represented by a written note, it will be capital gain. Otherwise, gain from the repayment of a loan will be ordinary income. However, if the basis in the loan is restored before the loan is repaid, no income will be recognized.

Compensation

The profits earned by an S Corporation are taxed to the shareholder/employee either as their share of the profits flowing through the S Corporation or as deductible (to the corporation) compensation paid to the shareholder. In most cases there will not be different tax consequences to the shareholders whether the income is salary or simply the shareholders' share of the S Corporation taxable income.

Tax Tip

If there is a risk that the S Corporation status may be terminated for any reason, it is preferable to have the income of the S Corporation paid to the shareholder/employees as salary, rents, or other corporate business expenses. Then, if the S Corporation status is terminated, the resulting regular corporation might not be left with much taxable income on which a corporate income tax must be paid.

In addition, it may be beneficial to have the income distributed as salary if doing so results in greater deductible contributions to a qualified pension plan (see Chapter Seven on Deferred Compensation).

On the other hand, salary payments are subject to employment taxes which may cause more tax to be paid than if the income flowed through to the shareholders other than as salary.

Example

Smart, Inc., an S Corporation, earns $100,000 before salary payments to its two shareholders. The entire $100,000 is paid to the shareholders as salary. It was subsequently determined that Smart, Inc. did not qualify as an S Corporation. There is no corporate tax on the federal level as a result of the failure to qualify as an S Corporation. If only $50,000 been paid as salary and $50,000 in profit flowed through to the shareholders, the corporation would have paid tax on $50,000.

If the S Corporation has a loss for the year, the payment of too much salary, rents, etc., to the shareholder/employees may result in losses flowing through to the shareholder/employee that cannot be taken. As we explained above, an S Corporation shareholder can only deduct losses to the extent of the shareholder's basis in the S Corporation stock or debt.

Important

One unfortunate aspect of S Corporation status is that an individual who owns 2% or more of stock of an S Corporation cannot exclude such employee fringe benefits as payments for group term life insurance, health and accident insurance, certain death benefits, and certain meals and lodging paid by the employer/S Corporation. The loss of the premiums paid on health insurance may be a substantial detriment to S Corporations that are not very substantial in terms of profit.

Points to Remember

1 In most cases, an S Corporation should pay as much salary to the shareholders as possible. In the event that S Corporation status is inadvertently terminated, the resulting regular corporation will not be stuck with as much tax liability.

2 However, the payment of too much salary may result in an S Corporation loss that cannot be deducted by shareholders because they do not have enough basis in the S Corporation.

3 A 2% or more shareholder of an S Corporation loses the tax benefits of the S Corporation paying certain fringe benefits.

There are several benefits to S Corporation status. Regular corporations using the cash basis method of accounting for tax purposes and the accrual basis method of accounting for book purposes may be subject to an alternative minimum tax at a 20% rate on one-half of the excess of the book income (earnings and profits starting in 1990) over the taxable income. This book/tax alternative minimum tax preference item is not applicable to S Corporations or shareholders of S Corporations. Also, regular corporations must switch to the accrual method of accounting when their gross receipts for a period of time average more than $5 million. S Corporations are not required to switch to the accrual method of accounting pursuant to this requirement. The ability to use the cash receipts and disbursements method of accounting may be a substantial benefit. Quite often, corporations on the accrual basis do not have the cash to pay the tax determined on the accrual basis.

Currently, the individual maximum income tax rate is lower than the corporate maximum income tax rate. It is possible that the individual rate will increase; but in the near future it is unlikely that it will exceed the corporate rate.

As indicated previously, regular corporations may not be able to deduct compensation and rents, etc., paid to shareholder/employees if the payments are in excess of a reasonable amount. The disallowed salary or rents may result in a corporate level tax. This unreasonable salary and corporate level tax generally will not exist for S Corporations.

Points to Remember

S Corporation status allows an entity to continue on the cash basis method of accounting, may eliminate the book/tax alternative minimum preference. Also, individual tax rates are lower than corporate rates. Finally, double taxation in many situations may be prevented when salary or rent paid to a shareholder/employee is deemed to be unreasonable by the tax authorities.

S Corporation status generally allows for an easier ultimate sale of the business by the owners. Since there generally is not a corporate level tax for S Corporations, the assets can be sold free of any corporate level tax. This makes disposition of the business easier, as a buyer might not want to buy the corporation and its potential liabilities that could be subsequently discovered. If the entity were a regular corporation and the buyer buys assets of the corporation (rather than the corporate stock), there would be a corporate level tax as well as a shareholder level tax when the sales proceeds are distributed to the shareholder.

Detriments of S Corporation status include: more restrictive estate planning opportunities, the inability of an S Corporation shareholder to borrow from a qualified pension or profit sharing plan sponsored by the corporation, and more professional time will have to be spent on transactions to determine that they do not inadvertently terminate S Corporation status. An existing corporation that uses the LIFO method of accounting and elects S Corporation status may have to recapture some of the prior LIFO benefits.

Important

Federal/State S Corporation Tax Law Differences

Some states such as California, impose a corporate level tax even on S Corporations. This is computed as if the corporation were not an S Corporation. In California the 2.5% S Corporation level rate is substantially lower than the regular 9.3% rate for non-S Corporations.

Some states impose corporate minimum tax that must be paid by all corporations including S Corporations. In California the minimum tax is $600 in 1989, and $800 in 1990 and thereafter. The California corporate tax is the higher of the tax on taxable income at the 2.5% S Corporate rate (9.3% for regular corporations) or the fixed sum ($600, or $800) minimum tax that is applicable for the year.

Example

If an S Corporation has taxable income of $1,000 in 1989, computed as if it were a regular Corporation, only $96 of regular corporate tax would be due. However, since the minimum tax for that year is $600, that is the amount which must be paid.

The total California tax on S Corporation income is 11.8%. It consists of the 2.5% corporate tax and the maximum individual tax rate that a shareholder must pay on his/her distributive share of the S Corporation income.

Tax Tip

The optimum tax planning objective in states that levy some sort of tax at the S corporation level is to strip out the earnings of the

S Corporation through expenses such as salary and rent that are deductible to the corporation. Of course, unreasonable compensation and rent payments will not be deductible.

In California if the entity were not an S Corporation, the corporation would pay a tax of 9.3% on its taxable income. Even with a 2.5% tax on the S Corporation, there is tax savings and tax benefits for California purposes from electing S Corporation status.

For California purposes, the shareholder's portion of the income flowing through the S Corporation is not reduced by the 2.5% tax levied at the S Corporation level.

Caution

Cal Corp. is an S Corporation that earned $100,000 before compensation payments to its two equal shareholders. $100,000 should be paid to the shareholders as salary or reimbursement of expenses before year end. The S Corporation will not have net taxable income and, therefore, will not have to pay the 2.5% California S Corporation income tax.

Example

A federal S election is generally treated as a State S election; however, starting in 1990 the California Tax Authorities must be appraised of the federal S election. This must be done on Form 5560 (CA) within the time period for making a federal election for a particular year. A $500 penalty may be assessed for failure to timely file the form.

A corporation may elect out of being treated as an S Corporation for State purposes although it is an S Corporation for federal purposes. However, the reverse may not be true. To qualify as an S Corporation for State purposes, it **must** be a federal S Corporation.

Important

The alternative minimum tax does not apply to S Corporations for State or federal purposes.

Important

For California purposes, 50% of the net operating loss incurred by an S Corporation can be carried forward and used to offset income in subsequent S Corporation years for purposes of determining the amount of income subject to the 2.5% tax. The carryover can only be made from income years in which an S Corporation election was in effect. As of 1988 the amount of income flowing through an S Corporation for California tax purposes is computed using the individual depreciation methods (as opposed to corporate depreciation methods).

As under federal rules, many states have a built-in gains tax for S Corporations. The tax only applies, however, to gains from sources within the state.

1   There now is substantial conformity in the federal and State tax rules for S Corporations.

Points to Remember

2   However, in some States such as California an S Corporation still must pay a 2.5% tax on its taxable income computed as if it were not an S Corporation.

3 A valid federal S election usually serves as a valid California S election although in California for elections made for taxable years beginning January 1,1990 or later, form 5560 (CA) must be filed with the California Tax Authorities.

See Chart 2 in Appendix for a list of states that have some form of S Corporation status. Some states accept a federal S Corporation election (Form 2553) as a valid state election while other states require that a separate election form be filed with the state tax authorities. States that allow a federal S election to be treated as a valid state election may allow the corporation to elect not to be an S Corporation in the state (even though it is an S Corporation for federal purposes). It may be advantageous to be an S Corporation for federal purposes but not for state purposes in certain situations.

Example

In December 1990, corporation Big Profit elects to be treated as an S Corporation for federal purposes for its calendar year beginning January 1991. During the 1990 tax year, Big Profit had a net operating loss that it could carry back for three years under the federal NOL carryback rules. However, the state in which Big Profit is located only allows operating losses to be carried forward (and not backward).

In the example, Big Profit should consider deferring S Corporation status for state purposes to a subsequent year so the NOL may offset subsequent year profits at the corporate level and avoid any state tax. A state S election effective in 1991 would prevent the corporation from using the NOL (regular corporation NOLs cannot be carried forward to S Corporation years) to offset the corporate profits which will flow through and be taxed at the shareholder level.

Vermont taxes a non-Vermont resident's share of an S Corporation's income at the corporation level. Thus, the S Corporation benefits only accrue to Vermont residents. Georgia, on the other hand, requires that nonresidents sign an agreement to pay Georgia individual income tax on the nonresident's share of the Georgia S Corporation's income. Illinois taxes S Corporation income at a 1.5% rate. Montana does not recognize S Corporation status for corporations not doing business in Montana. New York and Minnesota require a separate election for state purposes. In Massachusetts S Corporations with income over $6 million pay tax.

Points to Remember

There may be differences in S Corporation's treatment for federal and state purposes. Some states do not have a corporate and/or individual income tax; whereas, other states do not recognize S Corporation status for state purposes. Not all states that recognize S Corporation status conform exactly to the federal rules.

Partnerships

Partnerships

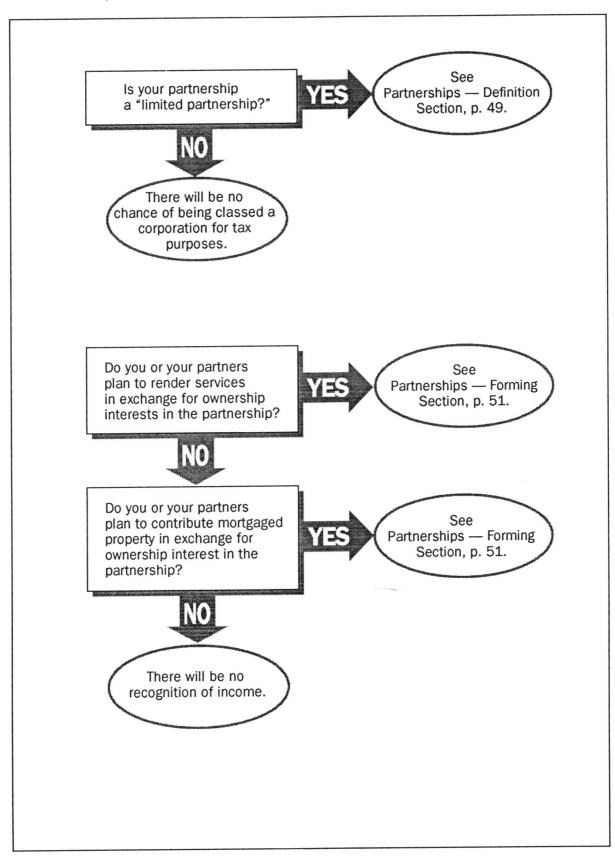

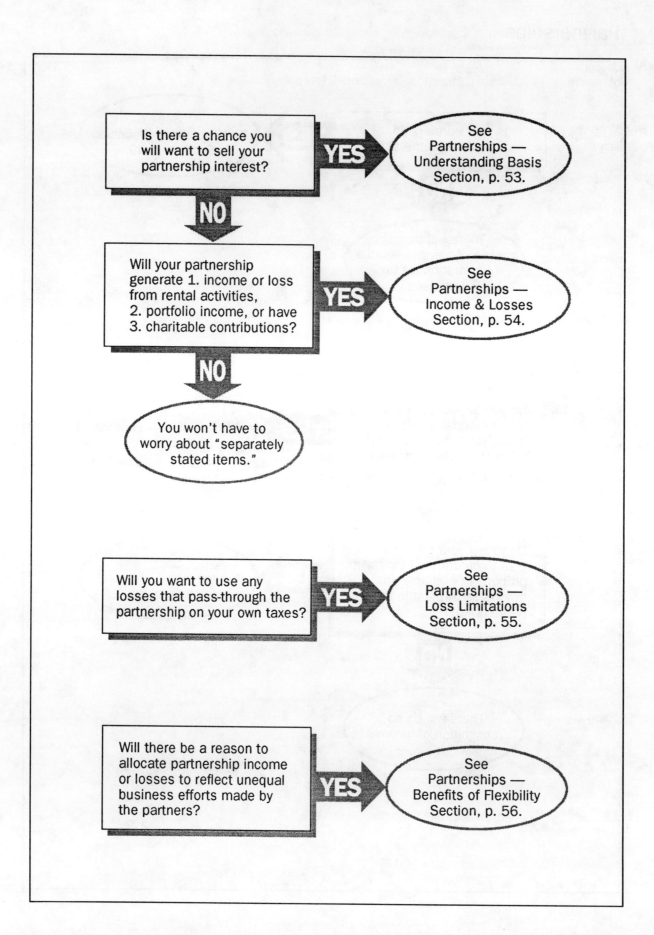

Is there a chance you will want to sell your partnership interest?

YES → See Partnerships — Understanding Basis Section, p. 53.

NO ↓

Will your partnership generate 1. income or loss from rental activities, 2. portfolio income, or have 3. charitable contributions?

YES → See Partnerships — Income & Losses Section, p. 54.

NO ↓

You won't have to worry about "separately stated items."

Will you want to use any losses that pass-through the partnership on your own taxes?

YES → See Partnerships — Loss Limitations Section, p. 55.

Will there be a reason to allocate partnership income or losses to reflect unequal business efforts made by the partners?

YES → See Partnerships — Benefits of Flexibility Section, p. 56.

The 1986 Tax Reform Act substantially increased the advantages of conducting business in the form of a partnership compared to the corporate form. One of these advantages is the elimination of double taxation. In addition, partnerships are generally very flexible in allocating the income and expenses to the various partners.

While partnerships have greater flexibility in this aspect, income and expenses cannot simply be allocated "willy-nilly." As you may already have guessed from our discussions of previous implementations of the tax laws, the IRS has made the fundamental principles for allowable allocations rather complicated.

Unlike S Corporations, partnerships never pay income taxes. A partnership files Form 1065 to calculate its taxable income which then flows through to, and is reported by, the partners. Form K-1 is attached to the 1065 to indicate the amounts of income, losses, and specially treated items that flow through to the various partners. Like the S Corporation, any item that has special treatment at the individual or other partner level is separately stated.

For example, the deduction for charitable contributions is limited for both corporations and individuals. Thus, partners' shares of charitable contributions are separately stated on the K-1.

The tax rules pertaining to the recognition of income, losses, and expenses are not unique for partnerships except in regard to transactions between partners and the partnership itself. If a partnership sells a widget for $100, the partnership has $100 of income as would any entity or taxpayer.

This chapter focuses on those situations which are unique to conducting business in the partnership form. These include such things as transactions between a partner and the partnership, the deduction for organization and syndication expenses incurred by a partnership, and other unique conditions.

Points to Remember

1 The 1986 Tax Reform Act enhanced the advantages of conducting business as a partnership relative to the corporate form.

   a Double taxation is avoided.
   b Partnerships are rather flexible in allocating income and expenses.
   c Partnerships never pay taxes. The income flows through to the partners.

2 A major drawback of the partnership form is the fact that partners may be exposed to liabilities that would not exist if the business were conducted in the corporate form.

Definition of Partnership

The definition of a partnership for tax purposes is much broader than for local law purposes. An arrangement or agreement that is not treated as a partnership under state law may not be treated as a partnership for both federal and state income tax purposes.

The formation of a partnership does not require an execution of a formal partnership agreement but merely the intent to conduct business in a manner that is a partnership.

There are two kinds of partnerships. In a "general partnership," each partner is responsible for the total debt of the partnership. The alternative is a limited partnership. If a limited partnership is properly formed, none of the limited partners will be responsible for debts and expenses of the partnership. The general partner will be totally responsible for such debts and expenses.

On the other hand, entities that may be treated as partnerships under California law may not be treated as partnerships for tax purposes. In some situations, entities that are actually partnerships for legal purposes are treated as corporations for tax purposes. This latter case can have rather severe financial consequences. Therefore, it is very important to secure knowledgeable professional tax advice on these issues.

Important

Normally, a partnership will only be treated as a corporation for tax purposes if it is a limited partnership that has improperly limited its liability because a general partner does not have sufficient capital or assets.

As you probably expect by now, the tax rules only vaguely define the term partnership. It is any joint venture which is not a corporation, trust, or estate. There must be two or more parties, and the parties must not have incorporated their joint effort.

Caution

Merely sharing expenses does not constitute a partnership. Also simple co-ownership of property does not result in a partnership for tax purposes.

A partnership does exist though if co-owners of real estate lease the real estate and also provide services to the occupants either directly or through agents.

There are essentially two key issues in determining whether an entity is a partnership or not. The first pertains to specific elections that must be made by the partnership on the partnership tax return. If the principals of an arrangement do not know they are a partnership, they will not file a partnership tax return. This may result in their losing the benefit of certain potentially valuable tax benefits.

The other issue concerns a partnership not being considered such for tax purposes. If an entity is treated as a corporation rather than a partnership for tax reasons, there may be substantial tax consequences at the corporate level.

Example

E & W were conducting the business of renting an office building. As part of the leasing agreement, they also provided secretarial and clerical support for the tenants. The individuals reported one-half of the profits and losses of the operation and

Example cont.

business on their respective 1040 forms. The business acquired new property each year, and the individuals elected on their separate individual tax returns to expense $10,000 of the property rather than capitalize and depreciate it.

The IRS and Franchise Tax Board audited the individual income tax returns for the two partners and determined that leasing the property and providing the secretarial services amounted to conducting business as a partnership for tax purposes. But because the election to expense the property was not made on a partnership return for the business, the partners could not expense the cost of the new property but had to capitalize and depreciate it.

If they had filed a partnership return and made the proper election, the partners could have expensed the cost of some of the assets.

Example

Able, Baker, Charlie, and Dog formed a limited partnership. Dog is a corporation and is the general partner of the limited partnership. Dog has minimal assets and virtually a zero net worth. The partnership reports $100,000 of taxable income for the first year of operations. None of cash from the operations is distributed to the partners, and there are no payments for services rendered by the partners.

The IRS and FTB audited the partnership and determined that, for tax purposes, it is not a partnership but is to be treated as a corporation. The reason for this is that the entity has limited liability due to the fact that the general partner has nominal or no net worth as well as other attributes of the limited partnership agreement. ABCD must pay a corporate tax on its $100,000 of taxable income. When the income, less corporate tax, is ultimately distributed to the owners, they will have to pay individual income tax. Thus, there is double taxation that could have been avoided had the owners recognized the issue and properly capitalized the corporate general partner.

Points to Remember

1   If two parties plan to conduct business as a partnership, it most likely will be treated as a partnership for tax purposes.

2   Some limited partnerships which fail to meet certain capitalization tests may be recharacterized as corporations or associations taxable as a corporation for tax purposes.

3   A joint venture of two parties who do not complete the legal partnership paperwork, may be treated as a partnership for tax purposes.

4   The risk of being classified as an association or corporation rather than a partnership is that there could be double taxation.

Forming a Partnership

Generally there is no gain or loss recognized for tax purposes when a partnership is formed and assets are contributed to the partnership by the partners. However, there are two main exceptions to this rule. The first is related below under "CAUTION." A second major exception has to do with contributing assets with mortgage balances.

Caution

If a partner renders services to the partnership in exchange for an interest in the partnership, that partner may have taxable income to the extent of the fair market value of the partnership interest received.

Example

Joe Boring, the Accountant for Fun Products Partnership, agrees to furnish accounting services to the partnership in exchange for a 10% interest in the partnership. The 10% interest is structured as capital and profits of the partnership. This means that Mr. Boring will receive 10% of the partnership's net worth should it be liquidated. With this arrangement Mr. Boring has immediate taxable income in the amount of the fair market value of the 10% partnership interest.

The partnership can deduct the value of the 10% interest if the services are to be rendered within one year. If the services are to be rendered over three years, the partnership must capitalize the value and deduct it pro rata over a three year period.

If a partner contributes property with a mortgage in excess of the tax basis of the property contributed, the partner must recognize income by the amount the mortgage is in excess of the tax basis of the property contributed.

Example

Bill Bucks contributes real estate worth $100,000 subject to a $50,000 mortgage to the Bucks/Cash 50/50 partnership. Bill's basis in the real estate is zero because he has owned the property for a long time and has depreciated it to a zero basis. Charlie Cash contributed $50,000 in cash to the partnership. Bill has taxable income as a result of this transaction of $25,000.

The gain is the amount of the mortgage in excess of the adjusted basis of the property less the one-half of the mortgage which Bill is still responsible for as a 50/50 partner.

Points to Remember

1   There is generally no gain or loss on the formation of a partnership.

    a   However, if a partner receives a partnership interest for services, income will be recognized.

    b   Also, if a partner contributes property with a mortgage in excess of the adjusted basis of the property, income will be recognized by the contributing partner.

Syndication Expenses

The legal, accounting, and other expenses of forming a partnership must be capitalized by the partnership. The partnership can make an election to deduct such capitalized amounts over a period of not less than 60 months.

If the partnership is an investment partnership and expenses are incurred to secure investors for the partnership, such syndication or selling expenses are not deductible by the partnership.

1   Various legal, accounting and organization expenses must be capitalized by the partnership and amortized over 60 months.

2   Investment partnerships cannot deduct syndication or selling expenses.

Understanding Basis

The basis of a partner's interest in a partnership is the amount paid for the partnership interest — the amount of cash or the tax basis of other property contributed to the partnership. A partner's basis in a partnership is also increased in some instances by the partner's share of liabilities incurred by the partnership. Basis is important in determining gain from the sale of a partnership interest. Also, losses may only be taken by a partner to the extent of the partner's basis in the partnership.

The partner's basis in property contributed to the partnership carries over to the partnership. The partner's basis becomes the partnership's basis in the property. If the partner recognizes a gain on the contribution, the property's basis for the partnership is increased by such gain.

Generally, a partner's basis in the partnership is increased by the partner's share of taxable income of the partnership and tax exempt income earned by the partnership. It is decreased by distributions from the partnership and losses flowing through the partnership to the partner.

A partner's basis can also be increased or decreased because of debt incurred or paid off by the partnership. A partner's basis is increased by the partner's share of additional debt incurred by the partnership. It is decreased by the repayment of such debt.

John Boring (Joe's brother) contributes $20,000 to Movie Star Partnership in exchange for a 20% interest in the partnership. The partnership has debt of $100,000. John's basis in the partnership is the $20,000 he contributed plus his share ($20,000) of the $100,000 debt incurred by the partnership. Thus, John can deduct $40,000 of losses flowing through the partnership because he has $40,000 of basis.

Example

If John sold his partnership interest for $200,000, his basis would be $40,000 and his gain would be computed as following.

	Amount
Sales Price	$200,000
Share of debt forgiven	$ 20,000
Total Sales Price	$220,000
Basis	$ 40,000
Gain from Sale of Partnership interest	$180,000

As you can be seen from the example, the debt provides basis in the partnership. However, the amount of proceeds deemed received by the partner is increased by the share of the partnership debt for which the selling partner is no longer responsible.

Points to Remember

1   A partnership's basis in its assets is the price it pays for the assets or the tax basis of the asset of the partner who contributed it to the partnership.

2   A partner's basis in the partnership is the amount of cash paid for the partnership interest or the tax basis of property contributed to the partnership.

3   A partner's basis is increased by the partner's share of liabilities and income. It is decreased by a reduction in the partner's share of liabilities and losses.

Understanding Partnership Income or Losses

The operating profits and losses of the partnership are reported by the partnership. They flow through to the various partners. Some items are separately stated by the partnership and flow through separately to the partners.

Example

A partnership has $100,000 of taxable income which is to be allocated to its ten partners. In arriving at the $100,000, $10,000 was deducted as a charitable contribution. Amounts flowing through to the partners as operating profits are $110,000, and $10,000 is separately stated as a charitable contribution. Thus, each of the ten equal partners would report $11,000 in operating income from the partnership and a $1,000 charitable contribution. The charitable contribution can be deducted on the individual partner's tax returns, subject to various limitations for charitable contributions.

Items that are separately stated and are not part of the operating profits or losses of the partnership include, among other things:

- Income or loss from a rental real estate activity
- Income or loss from other rental activities
- Portfolio income and elements thereof
- Charitable contributions

A partnership must generally have the taxable year of its partners. If the partners are individuals, the partnership must have a calendar year. If the partnership consists of two corporations as partners with the same fiscal year end, the partnership must use that fiscal year end.

A partnership may use other than a calendar year end even though all the partners are individuals using a calendar year end, if the partnership can establish a business purpose for doing so.

A partnership, like an S Corporation, may use a fiscal year end if it makes deposits with the tax authorities. The tax deposits are intended to represent the value of tax deferral that is obtained by the partners because of the ability to use a fiscal year.

In most cases, it is not advisable to use the deposit approach for securing a fiscal year that is different from the calendar year because the money does not earn interest. Also the deposit is not counted as part of the taxes paid by the partners. And finally, the partners must pay income tax on their share of the partnership income even though the partnership has made a deposit.

Tax Tip

1   Profits or losses are reported on a partnership return. They are distributed to the partners and accounted for on IRS Form K-1 for each partner.

2   Certain items of the partnership, such as charitable contributions and other tax sensitive items, are separately broken out on the Form K-1.

3   A partnership usually must have the same tax year as its partners.

Points to Remember

Loss Limitations

Losses that flow through to a partner can only be deducted to the extent the partner has basis in the partnership. If the loss is in excess of the partner's basis, the loss is suspended and carried forward until the partner acquires additional basis in the partnership.

At-risk rules apply to partnerships (as well as individuals and small corporations). Under the at-risk rules, a loss cannot be taken unless the taxpayer is "at-risk" or deemed to be at risk. At-risk generally means the partner must be liable for the full amount of the loss. If the taxpayer is not liable, the loss is suspended and carried forward until the taxpayer becomes at-risk.

Joe is a partner in the Debt Dodgers partnership. His share of the partnership's loss is $50,000 for tax year 1990. However, because of an agreement with partnership debtors and other parties, Joe will not be responsible for paying for any part of the loss. Since Joe is not at-risk with respect to the loss, he cannot take the loss until such time he becomes at-risk.

Example

1   Before you can deduct a loss flowing through from a partnership, you must meet three tests:

a   You must have basis in the partnership.
b   You must be at risk with respect to the amount of loss.
c   You must materially participate in the partnership's activity. (p.86)

Points to Remember

The sale of a partnership interest generally results in a capital gain or loss to the partner. However, if the partnership has unrealized receivables or appreciated inventory, some of the gain from the sale of the partnership may be treated as ordinary income.

Sales and Distributions of Partnership Interests

Example

Marvin Smart, an accountant, sells his 10% interest in Successful Accounting International partnership for $300,000. One-half of the sales price is attributable to bills that have been sent to clients by the partnership but not collected and not reported as taxable income. $150,000 of the gain from the sale of the partnership interest will be treated as ordinary income because of the unrealized receivables.

Important

In sharp contrast to corporations, gains or losses are not reported by a partner or partnership if cash or assets are distributed to a partner. However, gain is recognized if a partner receives cash from a partnership in excess of the partner's adjusted basis in the partnership.

Tax Tip

Care should be taken to prevent cash from being distributed to a partner in certain situations. In most cases, adverse tax consequences are prevented by including a clause in the partnership agreement stating that distributions are only "draws," or loans, from the partnership if the amount of the distribution exceeds the partner's tax basis.

Losses may be recognized by a partner in limited situations when cash, unrealized receivables, and inventory are the only items distributed to the partner in liquidation of a partnership interest.

Points to Remember

1   The sale of a partnership interest results in a capital gain or loss unless the partnership has unrealized receivables or appreciated inventory. In that case, a portion of the distribution is considered ordinary income for tax purposes.

2   Distributions of property including cash from a partnership are generally tax free. This is a substantially different situation than with corporations. It obviously is one of the benefits of the partnership form of business.

The Benefits of Flexibility

One of the advantages of conducting business as a partnership is that the income or losses of the partnership may be allocated to the partners to reflect business efforts made by the partners. This means that a partnership does not have to allocate its income 50/50 to partners who each own 50%.

The allocation of the profits or losses to the partners must be made pursuant to the partnership agreement. The partnership agreement may be oral or written. It may be amended for any taxable year prior to the due date (without extension) of the partnership's tax return (April 15 for a calendar-year partnership).

This means that the allocation of the profits or losses can be made after year end when the books are closed, profits determined, and the relative efforts of the partners are agreed upon. The partnership agreement is then amended to reflect the proper allocation.

Big Time Service Partnership has $1 million of taxable income for the period ending December 31, 1990. The three partners have until April 15, 1991, to agree how the income will be allocated among the partners. One partner may get more income (greater than 33%) because he/she worked more hours, generated more new customers, or contributed in some other manner.

Example

The allocation of partnership income and losses must have "substantial economic effect." You cannot allocate the income solely to take advantage of the tax laws. All the income of the partnership cannot be allocated to one partner who otherwise has a tax loss for the year if it's understood that all income will be allocated to other partners in subsequent years.

Caution

A partner reports his/her share of the partnership income or loss in the tax year in which the partnership year ends.

Important

1   Partnerships have a certain amount of leeway in allocating the income or losses to the various partners.

Points to Remember

2   There must be a valid business reason to allocate the income or losses other than on a pro rata basis.

Partnerships composed of several members of the same immediate family may provide opportunities for tax savings. However, because of the obvious tax advantages, these family partnerships are closely reviewed by the tax authorities.

Family Partnership

In a family partnership in which capital (cash, real estate, etc.) produces a material part of the income earned by the partnership, the income attributable to such capital must be allocated to the owners of the capital interests in the partnership.

Income cannot be allocated to younger family members in a lower tax bracket simply to save taxes. Also, the income allocated to a partner must reflect the value of services rendered by the various partners.

1   A partnership consisting of family members is closely scrutinized by the tax authorities. This is to ensure that income and assets are not shifted from wealthier partners to less affluent partners.

Points to Remember

CHAPTER FIVE

State Taxation
of Business Income

State Taxation of Business Income

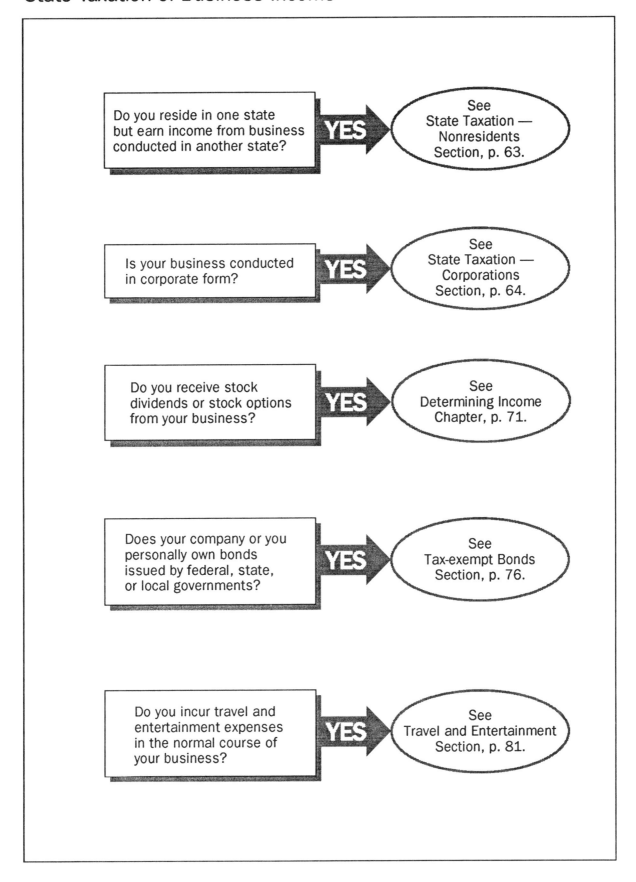

States that have a personal income tax will tax their residents on their worldwide income. (See Appendix IV for a list of the personal income tax rates in various states.) If you live in New York and earn income in California from selling goods and services in California you will have to pay tax in New York on the income earned in California. The state where you live will generally allow you an offsetting credit for taxes paid to another state. The credit is generally limited to the proportionate tax in the state of residence on the income earned in the other state.

State Taxation for Residents and Nonresidents

Joe Engineer who lives in California is in the equipment repair business and provides those services in another state. The income earned from business done out of California is subject to tax in the other state because services are provided there. If $10,000 is earned in the other state and $100 is paid in taxes to that state on the income, California tax will be offset by $100. On the other hand, Joe would be limited in how much credit he would get for paying the other state's taxes. If the other state taxed the $10,000 income to the tune of $1200 and California's tax was $930, Joe could only offset the $930. He would not earn an additional credit for the balance.

Example

A nonresident of a state is generally only taxed on income earned in the state. For example, a resident of Nevada doing equipment repair in California would be subject to California taxation on the income earned from performing the services in the state. Usually nonresidents of a state are not taxed on dividend and interest income even if paid by individuals or businesses resident in the state. Nonresidents are taxed on income from real property and tangible personal property located in a state.

As you can see, it is important to know an individual's residency status. You are generally considered a resident of a state if you are in the state for other than a temporary purpose. If you are in California for no more than six months during the year and maintain a permanent home in another state, you will generally be considered a nonresident *unless* you conduct business in California.

There is a presumption that you are a California resident if you reside in the state for more than nine months. Even then it is possible to prove you are not a resident by showing the existence of extensive business and property ownership outside California. However, it is an uphill battle convincing the California tax authorities that you are not a resident if you spend nine months in the state. In most such cases, you are subject to California taxation of your worldwide income.

You are a resident of California if you reside permanently in California though live temporarily outside the state. This means that if you have a permanent residence in California but spend three months of the year vacationing or even doing business in another state, you are still deemed to be a resident of California. You are taxed by the state on all your income.

An individual is a resident of New York if his permanent home is in New York or he spends more than 183 days in a taxable year in New York. Other states have similar definitions of resident or non-resident status.

Points to Remember

1 An individual resident of a state will be taxed on all his/her worldwide income by the state.

2 A nonresident is taxed only on income earned in a state including income from sources located in the state such as rental property.

3 A nonresident of a state is generally not taxed by the state on dividends or interest even if paid by resident entities of the state.

4 A resident of a state is generally any person who is in the state for other than a temporary purpose.

5 An individual who spends less than six months of the year in a state is not generally considered a resident.

State Taxation for Corporations

A state corporate franchise tax is imposed upon corporations organized in the state and on corporations organized in other states if the corporation does business in the state. (See Appendix V for a list of corporate income tax rates in various states.) "Doing business" is tax jargon. If a corporation seeks to profit from its activities in a state, it is "doing business." If a corporation headquartered in another state is only collecting dividend and interest income in a state, the corporation is not considered to be "doing business" in a state. It will not be subject to the state's franchise tax.

Corporations organized in a state which are not subject to the state franchise tax, as explained above, are still subject to the state's corporate income tax if the corporation has income from sources within such state. For example, a corporation organized in another state may pay California income tax (rather than franchise tax) if it owns California property and leases it to tenants on a net lease basis. "Net lease" means the tenant of the California property pays all the taxes and associated expenses with respect to the property.

Important

If a corporation is subject to a state's franchise tax, it is necessary to determine how much of its income is subject to state taxes. This is done by an "apportionment" formula. Once the income of the corporation is known, the percentage of the income subject to taxation by a state is based on the ratio of "factors" such as, property, payroll, and sales located or taking place in the state to the total property, payroll, and sales of the corporation. Property is located in a state if it is physically situated there. Payroll is in a state if the employee works in the state. Sales are in the state, generally, if the distribution of the property is within the state. If the entire property, payroll, and sales factors are in a state, all of the income will be taxed by that state. Many states have adopted the Uniform Division of

Income for Tax Purposes Act ("UDITPA"). This generally results in states using the same or similar factors for apportioning business income. (See Appendix VI for a list of states using UDITPA.)

> XYZ Corporation is doing business in California (it does not matter whether it is incorporated in California or in another state). It has 50% of its payroll, 30% of its sales, and 10% of its property in California (a total of 90%). 30% of XYZ Corporation's taxable income (90% divided by 3) will be apportioned to California and taxed by California.

Example

If a corporation has non-business income, such as interest and dividends, that income is "allocated" to the state where the corporation has its commercial domicile (its corporate headquarters). That income is then taxed by that state. Income from tangible property not used in the business is usually taxed in the state where the property is located. A corporation generally is not required to pay state tax (for example, in California) on rental income from real property (or personal property) located in another state if the property is not used in the business that is conducted in California.

Points to Remember

1 A corporation is taxed by a state on the part of its business income earned in the state even if it is incorporated in another state.

2 Many states have adopted UDITPA — a uniform method for apportioning business income to various states.

3 Non-business income such as dividends and interest is taxed in the state where the corporation has its headquarters.

4 Non-business income from tangible property such as rental property is generally taxed in the state where the tangible property is located.

Determining Income and Deductible Expenses

Determining Income and Deductible Expenses

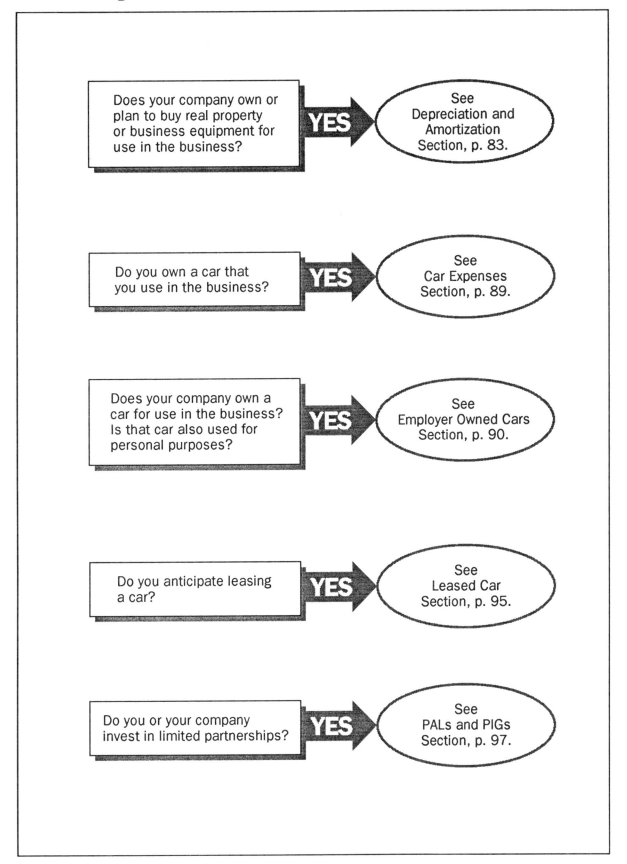

As Mortimer Caplan, a former Commissioner of the IRS stated, "There is one difference between a tax collector and a taxidermist — the taxidermist leaves the hide." The following material discusses the basic rules of determining taxable income and deductible expenses. It will also provide planning ideas and tips so you will be left with at least some hide.

Taxpayers are taxed on their gross income, less allowable deductions. Gross income is figured in essentially the same way for all taxpayers whether they are individuals, corporations, partnerships, estates, or trusts. Gross income is any income from whatever source it is derived. Income may be money or it may be some other form such as services or property. This simply means that if you receive stock in a corporation in exchange for providing services, you have gross income in the amount of the fair market value of the stock. If a plumber exchanges plumbing services with his/her accountant for accounting services, both the plumber and the accountant have gross income even though no cash or property was received.

Income

Income is received if a taxpayer has an increase in wealth attributable to a taxable event or transaction. The simple appreciation of stock or real estate does not constitute gross income even though it results in increased wealth.

There are specific exclusions preventing the taxation of income or increases in the wealth of an individual or business. Life insurance proceeds received on the death of an individual are excluded from gross income as well as certain employee benefits. Gifts, inheritances, and compensation for injury or sickness are also excluded.

Important

There must be a "realization" of income to be taxed. The Supreme Court ruled that when a shareholder received a dividend in the form of additional common stock of a corporation, there was no realization of income. This is because when you receive a stock dividend, your percentage ownership of the company's outstanding stock does not change even though you own more shares. The total number of shares in the company also increases leaving everyone with the same percentage of the total stock.

While stock dividends paid in additional shares are not taxable events, if you have an option to elect to receive the stock dividend in the form of additional shares or cash, it is treated as a "realization" of income. You will be taxed just as though you received a cash dividend.

Caution

A taxpayer is not taxed on amounts received as an agent or nominee for another taxpayer. If an individual has legal title to shares of stock as an agent or nominee for another person (for whatever reason), the agent will not be taxed on the dividends or interest paid on that stock. The true or beneficial owner recognizes the income and is taxed on it. There may be a problem convincing the tax authorities that property is held as a nominee or agent for another. Be sure that you have completed the appropriate paperwork and have thorough records in case the question does arise. You may want to file Form 56 (Notice of Fiduciary Relationship) with the tax authorities to tell them you are not the beneficial owner of certain assets.

Income from community property is generally taxed one-half to each spouse. If property is jointly held by other than married couples, the income is generally divided equally among the co-owners.

Example   Joe and Bill are each 50/50 owners of 100 shares of Bic Bank stock. The stock paid a dividend of $50. Each co-owner must report one-half of the dividend income.

In certain situations, the tax authorities will "impute" income to a taxpayer. This means that they will declare that the individual (or corporation or partnership) received taxable income. An example of imputed income would be an interest free loan from an employer to an employee. The employee is treated as having income in the amount of the interest that would have been paid if the loan had been a normal interest-bearing debt. The employee will also be treated as having paid interest — but may not be able to deduct all of such interest. (See Chapter Ten's discussion of interest deduction rules.)

Receipts attributable to deductions taken in prior years are not excludable. If an individual received a reimbursement of expenses previously deducted, such reimbursed expenses are includable in income to the extent previously deducted.

If an employer pays non-business expenses of an employee, the employee has taxable income. If an employer for business reasons (better company image) pays an employee's car expense, including monthly lease payments, the employee will have taxable income in the amount of payments made. This also applies if a corporation pays the personal expenses of a shareholder/employee. Income will be realized by the shareholder/employee. The income will be either compensation for services (and thus subject to income tax withholding) or treated as a dividend paid by the corporation to the shareholder/employee. In both cases the employee has income. If the payment is considered a dividend rather than compensation, the corporation cannot deduct it as a business expense.

Example   Corporation Tango reimburses the expenses of its 100% shareholder/employee. The IRS audits the corporate tax return and determines that the expenses were personal expenses of the employee rather than business expenses. The employee has income in the amount of the payments made for personal benefit of the employee.

The tax authorities will contend that the payments are really dividends that are not deductible by the corporation. The employee may contend that the payments were compensation either as an employee or independent contractor and thus deductible by the corporation. In either event the employee has income.

Employees realize income to the extent they purchase stock from their employer at a bargain price. For example, if you are allowed to purchase stock from your employer for $100 per share when the fair market value is $200 per share, you have $100 of income for each share purchased.

Important

Quite often corporate employers want to give employees options to buy stock in the company. This serves as an incentive to motivate the employee and does not require a cash payment on the part of the employer. The difference between the fair market value of the option and the amount paid for the option is income **at the time the option is received.** If the option cannot be valued at the time of receipt, as is usually the case, the difference between the option price and the fair market value of the stock at the time the option is exercised is ordinary income.

John Doe received a stock option to purchase 1,000 shares of XYZ Corporation for $5 per share. The fair market value of the option on the date granted was $2 per share. Mr. Doe exercised the option after one year when the fair market value of the stock is $15 per share. Mr. Doe held the stock for 13 months and then sold it for $35 per share.

Example

Mr. Doe realized $2,000 of ordinary income on the day the option was granted ($2 X 1,000 shares). He does not recognize income on the exercise of the option.

He has a basis in the stock of $7 ($2 recognized as income and $5 paid for the stock). When he sold the stock, he realized a long term capital gain of $28 per share ($35 sales price less $7 basis) for a total of $28,000 ($28 X 1,000 shares).

Bob Smith-Jones received a stock option to purchase 1,000 shares of ABC International stock at $5 per share. The option did not have an ascertainable value at the time it was granted. Mr. Smith-Jones exercised the option 18 months later when the stock was selling at $10 a share. He realized $5,000 of ordinary income at that time ($10 value per share less $5 paid per share x 1,000). He paid taxes for that income in the year it was realized.

Example

One year later Mr. Smith-Jones sold the stock at $25 per share. He realized a $15,000 long term capital gain on the sale of the stock ($25 sales price, less $10 basis per share x 1,000). He was liable for taxes on that gain in the year it was realized.

As you can see from our examples, it is usually better to receive a stock option that can be valued or exercise a stock option when the value of the stock is low or equal to the option price. The corporate employer will be entitled to a deduction equal to the ordinary income recognized by the employee at the time the employee recognizes the income.

Tax Tip

Rather than give stock options, a corporate employer may transfer stock to an employee on the condition that the employee must continue working for the corporation for a stated period of time. During that period the stock proportionally vests in (i.e., becomes the property of) the employee. For example, an employer might transfer 1,000 shares of stock to an employee on the condition that the employee work for the company an additional five years. One-fifth of the stock will vest in the employee each year during the five-year period.

The employee realizes income each year as 200 shares of the stock (20% of the initial 1,000 shares) is vested in the employee. The amount of income is the fair market value of the stock at the time it vests. Alternatively, at the time the employee receives the stock (subject to the employment conditions), he/she may elect to declare as income the excess of the fair market value of the stock at that time over the amount the employee pays for the stock.

Caution

The election of the tax treatment of the restricted stock must be made within 30 days of the receipt of the restricted stock.

Tax Tip

Usually in instances of restricted stock, if the stock is of nominal value, you should elect to immediately realize as income the excess of the fair market value of the stock over the amount you pay for it. This is because the election will not result in much income being recognized.

If the election is made and the stock is sold in the future, the difference between the amount included in income and the sales price of the stock will be capital gain. It will or will not be long term capital gain depending on how long the stock was held before it was sold. The employer will be entitled to a deduction when, and to the extent, the employee recognizes income.

Example

John's wife, Jane Doe, works for Big Bucks Corporation and receives 1,000 shares of stock on January 1, 1990. In order to keep the 1,000 shares, she must work five years for the company. Each year, 200 shares of the stock are vested for her. She can do with the vested shares as she pleases. At the time the 1,000 shares of stock are transferred to her, Jane can elect to include the excess of its fair market value over what she will pay for the stock in her income. Or she will realize income in the amount of the value of the stock when the condition of continued employment expires.

If she does not make the election to include the requisite amount in her income when the initial transfer was made within the 30-day period, she must recognize income on December 31, 1990, in the amount of the fair market value of 200 shares of stock on that date.

Points to Remember

1   A determination of whether a taxpayer has gross income is generally not different whether the business is conducted as a sole proprietorship, partnership, or corporation.

2   Gross income is broadly defined. When wealth is increased due to a taxable event or transaction, there is gross income.

■ There must be a realization of the gross income. The mere increase in net worth of a person, partnership or corporation because property values such as real estate or stocks have appreciated does not constitute a "realization" of gross income.

3 The realization of gross income is not limited to cash receipts. The receipt of stock, other tangible property or even services in exchange for services results in gross income.

4 Income from jointly owned property is generally divided among the co-owners of the property. Income from community property is generally one-half recognized by each spouse.

5 In certain situations, income is imputed to a taxpayer. For example, an interest-free loan from an employer to an employee may be deemed receipt of income by tax authorities.

6 The receipt of stock from a corporate employer or stock options to purchase stock in a corporate employer may result in income to the employee.

As you can see, the tax authorities take a broad view as to what is considered income. Some even say that everything is income unless it is subject to a specific statutory or judicial exclusion. In this section, we discuss receipt of cash and/or other property that has value but is specifically excluded from taxation.

Exclusions from Gross Income

Damages received for personal injury are excluded from income. If a personal injury claim results in court-awarded damages or an out-of-court settlement, the money received is excluded from income. Therefore it is not taxed. Money received as damages for lost profits is taxed. However, generally punitive damages received after July 10, 1989, for other than physical injury or sickness is taxable.

Amounts received to compensate an employee for permanent bodily injury are excluded from income even if the premiums on the policies were paid by the employer. Amounts received under workers' compensation acts for medical expenses and/or medical disabilities resulting from personal injuries or sickness are excludable from income. See Chapter Two for a list of other fringe benefits that are excluded from income in various situations.

Money received as damages for personal slander and libel are not taxable. But if the damages are received for injury via slander or libel to one's business or profession, they are taxable.

A decedent's, or other beneficiary's, proceeds from a life insurance policy are excluded from gross income. Life insurance proceeds, though, may be subject to an estate tax based on assets owned by the decedent at the time of death (see Chapter Twelve for details on Gift, Estate, and Real Property Taxes).

If a corporation or partnership buys life insurance on an employee/owner of the corporation or partnership, the receipt of the life insurance proceeds by the corporation or partnership will not be taxable for regular income tax purposes.

Caution

Life insurance proceeds received by a corporation other than an S Corporation will, however, be subject to the corporate alternative minimum tax (see Alternative Minimum Tax — Corporations in this chapter).

Often small businesses will buy life insurance policies on owners in order to provide funds to buy out a deceased owner's share of the business. Key person insurance provides needed cash for the business during the period immediately following the death of an owner. Disability buy-out insurance may be purchased as well.

Example

ABC Corporation buys a $1 million life insurance policy on each of its two equal owners. The proceeds of the life insurance on the death of one owner will be used by the corporation to buy out the deceased owner's interest in the corporation. The life insurance proceeds will not be subject to the regular income tax but may result in an alternative minimum tax of $100,000.

Tax Tip

Owners of corporate businesses should acquire life insurance policies on their "partners" directly rather than through the business. In this way they can avoid the potential alternative minimum tax exposure.

Up to $5,000 is excluded from income if paid to a surviving spouse or the decedent's estate by an employer because of the death of the employee. This benefit is available to employee/shareholders of closely held corporations. The benefit is not available to a self-employed individual or to a partner in a partnership.

The value of property received as a gift or inheritance is excluded from taxable income. Often there is an uncertainty whether amounts are received as a gift or as compensation for rendering services to the transferring party.

For example, "tips" paid to people rendering a service such as waiters, bellhops, or hair stylists are taxable income. Although they are in the nature of a gift, tax authorities hold that tips are in reality payment for services rendered.

Tax-exempt Bonds

The federal government excludes from taxation interest from state and local debt instruments or obligations issued prior to August 7, 1986. The 1986 Tax Reform Act imposed significant limitations on the ability of state and local governments to issue tax-exempt bonds. Interest on some bonds is subject to the alternative minimum tax.

Caution

Before buying any municipal bond to earn tax-exempt interest, double-check with your tax or investment advisor to ensure the issue is indeed tax-exempt in your case for regular and alternative minimum tax purposes. This is a highly technical and complex area where some bonds do not meet the strict federal requirements for tax-exempt status.

Ida Investor received $10,000 in interest income in 1990. $5,000 was interest income from federal bonds, $2,500 was from qualified California bonds and $2,500 was from qualified bonds issued by the State of Missouri. For federal income tax purposes, Ida was only liable for taxes on the $5,000 of interest income from the federal obligations. For California tax purposes, Ida was liable only for taxes on the $2,500 of interest income from the Missouri obligations.

Example

Many states, such as, California, exclude interest received on federal obligations and their own state and local obligations. They may not exclude interest income from obligations issued by other states or their subdivisions.

From a tax standpoint, it is more advantageous, for example, for California residents to invest in California or California local government municipal bonds because no income tax will be paid on interest from such obligations. Don't make the mistake of making investments for tax reasons only. There are many non-tax related factors in any investment decision. For example, you should weigh risk and the rate of return offered by a state's tax-exempt bonds relative to the whole universe of alternative issues.

Corporate Considerations
Contributions to a corporation made by a shareholder are not taxable income to the corporation.

Important

In some situations contributions to a corporation by a non-shareholder are taxable. Subsidies paid or contributed to a corporation are taxable to the corporation. If a corporation receives a nontaxable contribution of cash from a non-shareholder, the basis of any property purchased with the money during the 12 month period following the contribution is reduced by the amount of the contribution. A corporation is not allowed to exclude the funds from income and take depreciation deductions on assets purchased with the funds. The basis of property other than cash contributed to a corporation by a non-shareholder is zero.

Employee Fringe Benefit Considerations
Meals and/or lodging furnished for the convenience of the employer is also excluded from the income of the employee. The meals must be served on the employer's "business premises" to qualify as excludable. Lodging must be on the employer's business premises and the employee must be required to accept such lodgings as a condition of employment. Business premises means a place where the employee performs a significant portion of duties or the employer conducts a significant portion of business.

Up to $5,000 of dependent care assistance provided by an employer may be excluded for an employee. This fringe benefit and many other "excludable" fringe benefits mentioned previously are only excludable if the benefits are provided on a nondiscriminatory basis to employees. The purpose of the nondiscrimination rule is to prevent employee/owners from taking advantage from such fringe benefits but not providing them to the nonowner employees.

Caution

Many fringe benefits that favor owners or highly compensated employees may not be excluded from income.

Fringe benefits offered under "cafeteria plans" may also be excluded. A cafeteria plan has nothing to with "doing lunch"! Rather the term has been coined to describe a combination of various employee benefits that may be offered by an employer. Employees cannot elect all the benefits offered in a cafeteria plan. Specific benefits are selected by employees to tailor the package to their particular circumstances.

Points to Remember

1   Life insurance proceeds received on the death of an individual are excluded from gross income.

2   Life insurance proceeds received by a corporation and used to buyout a shareholder are not subject to regular income tax but may be subject to an alternative minimum tax.

3   Although not subject to an income tax, life insurance proceeds may be subject to an estate tax.

4   The value of property received as a gift or an inheritance is not subject to income tax.

5   The federal government excludes from taxable income interest earned on bonds issued by state or local governments prior to August 7, 1986. Municipal bonds issued since then are also federally tax-exempt; however, there are exceptions.

6   Many states exclude from taxable income interest on federal government and their own state and local government bonds.

   ■   They may not exclude interest on bonds issued by other states or their subdivisions.

7   Compensation received for personal injury damages is generally excluded from income.

8   Meals and lodging furnished for the convenience of an employer are excluded as well as certain fringe benefits such as dependent care assistance.

Business Expenses

Business expenses are usually deductible whether the business is conducted in the form of a sole proprietorship, a corporation, or a partnership. If the business is conducted as a partnership or corporation, the income and business expenses will appear in the profit and loss statement on the tax returns filed by the organization. If the business is conducted as a sole proprietorship, the income and the expenses of such business will be reflected on the Schedule C which accompanies the individual income tax return of the owner.

A business can deduct all the ordinary and necessary expenses paid or incurred during the taxable year in carrying on any trade or business. However, if a cost is in the nature of a capital expenditure (e.g., purchase of equipment that has a useful life of more than one year), it must be deducted over a period of time (depreciated over its useful life). The purchase of property is clearly a capital expenditure which must be deducted as depreciation over a period of time. Other examples of capital expenditures include amounts paid to acquire property (commissions, recording fees, etc.), architectural plans, or legal fees and other costs incurred to form a corporation or partnership.

If an expenditure is made to prepay an item, a deduction should be taken over the period to which the prepayment relates, rather than in the year in which the prepayment is made.

Hard Rock Corporation paid three years of liability insurance in 1990. The payment must be "written off" or deducted over the three-year period to which it relates. The full prepayment cannot be deducted in 1990, the year paid.

Example

The terms "ordinary and necessary" and "carrying on a trade or business" are debated, often in a heated fashion, by tax practitioners and tax authorities. Generally, "ordinary and necessary" means expenses that are normal, usual, or customary. It may be ordinary and necessary even though it is only incurred "once in a blue moon."

In one important Supreme Court case, the issue of what was ordinary was addressed. In the case, a former officer of a bankrupt corporation wished to strengthen his own credit and to re-establish his relationship with the bankrupt company's former customers. After the formal bankruptcy of the corporation, he voluntarily paid certain creditors of the corporation. The Supreme Court denied his "business expense" deduction of the amounts paid to the creditors. They concluded that although the payment may have been necessary in the individual's trade or business, it was not ordinary. It was a capital expenditure to build a reputation.

But just to show how complex this area is, the Court held, in another case on somewhat similar facts, that comparable expenses were made to retain existing goodwill. The Court ruled these expenses **were** deductible as ordinary and necessary. They further concluded that these expenses were not capital expenditures.

Business expenses must be "reasonable" as well as ordinary and necessary. This requirement most often comes into play when the IRS moves to disallow the salaries paid to employee/shareholders on the grounds they were unreasonable in amount.

The reasonable amount issue is also often raised in the area of travel and entertainment expenses. The rule is that there can be no lavish entertainment expenses. What is a reasonable expense is a function of the business incurring the expense. For example, what is a reasonable entertainment expense for the Rockefellers may not be a reasonable entertainment expense for the Flintstones.

The reasonable amount argument is frequently raised by the tax authorities when a corporation pays rent to a shareholder for the use of real property or equipment. When expenses paid to or for the benefit of a shareholder are deemed to be unreasonable, they still will generate income to the shareholder. However, the income is dividend income rather than deductible corporate expenses like rental income or salaries.

Example

The I.M. Greedy Corporation is 100% owned by Patrick Piig. The corporation leases the real property used in the corporate business from Mr. Piig. It pays $10,000 per month rent. $120,000 is deducted on the corporate return each year. The tax return is audited and the IRS determined that only $60,000 was a reasonable amount to pay for the rental of the property. $60,000 of the payment will be reclassified as dividends which cannot be deducted by the corporation. Mr. Piig has $120,000 in income even though the IRS reclassifies the payments. Mr. Piig winds up with $60,000 in rental income and $60,000 in dividends from the company.

To reiterate, a deductible expenditure must be made in the process of carrying on a trade or business. To meet the carrying-on requirement, a trade or business must be intended as a profit-making venture. This provision is drawn to eliminate people using hobbies, where the chief motivation is pleasure rather than profit, to generate tax deductions. The most common tax disputes over the "carrying-on" requirements pertain to expenses incurred by businesses that are just starting but whose expenses were incurred before the business starts.

For a good illustration of the line dividing what type of expenses are deductible and which are not, consider the case of an aspiring doctor. Expenses incurred by a doctor prior to actually obtaining a license to practice are not considered to have been amassed while "carrying on" the trade or business of being a doctor. The expenses were incurred prior to the time the trade or business could begin legally. Therefore they are not deductible.

Note

Fines and penalties paid to the government are not deductible. Most businesses incur penalties like parking tickets. The tickets are considered penalties and are not deductible.

Illegal payments to public officials or employees are not deductible. Bribes and kickbacks made to nongovernment officials are not deductible if the bribe or kickback is illegal, and the payer is subject to punishment by the authorities.

Finally, distinguished from illegal payments is the deductibility of payments with respect to an illegal business. Generally, expenses such as rent of an illegal business are deductible. But the illegal expenses of an illegal business are not deductible. For example, rent paid to operate a illegal business such as a gambling hall would be deductible. But bribes paid to public officials to conduct the business would not be deductible.

1   The deduction of business expenses is essentially the same regardless of whether the business is conducted as a sole proprietorship, a corporation or a partnership.

2   The ordinary and necessary expenses of conducting the business are deductible.

3   The cost of acquiring equipment and other capital assets must be capitalized and recovered through depreciation deductions.

4   Prepaid expenses or expenses that pertain to a long period of time also must be capitalized and amortized over the period to which they relate.

5   Business expenses must be "reasonable in amount."

6   If a salary paid by a regular corporation is determined to be unreasonable by the tax authorities, the employee/shareholder still has the income but the corporation loses the benefit of a deduction. The proportion of the compensation that is considered unreasonable is deemed a dividend, which is not deductible.

7   Fines, penalties, bribes, and kickbacks are not deductible.

Points to Remember

Only 80% of entertainment expenditures are deductible. The 80% limit even applies to the cost of meals incurred in the course of travel away from home overnight. To add further confusion to the issue, not all entertainment expenses are 80% deductible. For example, transportation to and from a restaurant for a business meal is 100% deductible even though the cost of the business meal itself is only 80% deductible. Travel costs such as transportation and lodging are generally 100% deductible. We never said it made a lot of sense!

Travel and Entertainment

Miscellaneous business expenses such as travel and entertainment incurred by employees who are not reimbursed by their employer can only be deducted to the extent they exceed 2% of the employee's adjusted gross income.

Important

Entertainment expenses must be directly related to the active conduct of a trade or business. Club dues are deductible if the club is used primarily (more than 50% of the time) to further a taxpayer's business **and** the use of the club is directly related to the taxpayer's business. For California purposes, expenses incurred at a club and club dues are not deductible if the club discriminates based on race, color, or creed.

Important   A deduction will not be allowed merely for buying a meal for a customer, client, or prospective client. Business must be discussed shortly before, during, or after the meal. Make a note on what business was discussed in your appointment diary or on your expense receipt.

Business Meal, Travel & Entertainment Deductibility Checklist

Type of Expenditure	100%	80%	0%
BUSINESS MEALS			
"Quiet business meal," no business discussed			x
Lavish and extravagant meal			x
Lunch with employee, business discussed		x	
Lunch with employee, no business discussed			x
Lunch with customer, business discussed		x	
Lunch with customer, no business discussed			x
Lunch with customer on your road trip, no business discussed			
Customer's meal			x
Your meal		x	
Dinner for employee working overtime (small)	x		
Lunch ordered in for staff meeting (small)	x		
Lunch and dinner provided at or near cost to employees at			
employer-operated cafeteria	x		
Dinner for customer and spouse, no one else present			x
Transportation to/from restaurant for business meal	x		
ENTERTAINMENT			
Transportation to/from sporting event		x	
Ticket price for sporting event associated with business discussion		x	
Cover charge, taxes and tips		x	
Country club dues and fees, 40% of use for business entertaining			x
Country club dues and fees, 60% of use fees for business entertaining (60% portion)		x	
TRAVEL EXPENSES			
Transportation and lodging expenses	x		
Meals taken alone while away from home		x	

Table 6.1

Taxpayers must substantiate travel, meal, and entertainment expenses by keeping records that prove:

1   The amount of the expenditure
2   The date of the expenditure
3   The place of entertainment or destination of travel
4   The business purpose of the entertainment or travel
5   The business relationship of the person entertained

Maintain a chart of accounts that details and keeps a cumulative total of expenses that are subject to the 80% limitation. Refer to Table 5.1 for business meal, travel, and entertainment deductibility.

1   "Reasonable" travel and entertainment expenses are deductible subject to limitations.

2   Only 80% of most entertainment expenses is deductible.

3   Maintain records of travel and entertainment expenditures which show the amount, date, place, purpose of the expenditure, and the relationship to the party entertained.

Points to Remember

You would think that the computation of depreciation is rather simple. If you purchase an asset with an estimated useful life of five years, it would be logical to think that you could write off one-fifth of the asset each year. But the people who draw up the tax code don't go for anything that straightforward.

Depreciation and Amortization

Deductions for depreciation are very complicated because almost every year the tax rules change. For federal tax purposes, the amount of depreciation is drastically different, depending on whether the property was placed in service before 1981, after 1980 and before 1987, or after 1986. But it gets even worse. Although the basic rules remain the same for property placed in service after 1980 and before 1987, the useful life or recovery period of various types of property is significantly different, depending on exactly when the property was placed in service.

The California rules were generally the same as the federal rules until 1981 and are generally the same for individuals after 1986. The California rules essentially stated that "facts and circumstances" would determine the useful life of various assets but the depreciation method was defined. Starting in 1987 the federal and California rules for depreciation are basically the same for property placed in service after 1986 by individuals.[1,2]

---

[1] Depreciation Rules before 1981.

Depreciation was basically the same for California and for federal purposes for property placed in service before 1981. The rule stated that property could be depreciated over its useful life and could not be depreciated below a reasonable estimated salvage value. The depreciation method varied, based on whether the property was new or used when it was placed in service by taxpayer and whether it was personal property, residential or nonresidential real property. The most

Depreciation After 1986

For those of you who are interested, we have detailed the different approaches taken to depreciation in the pre-1981 phase and the 1981 to 1986 rules in footnotes one and two. We will concentrate our efforts here on the post-1986 rules.

The MACRS depreciation system replaced the ACRS depreciation system. The new MACRS rules apply to property placed in service after 1987 but may be elected for most depreciable property placed in service after July 31, 1986. Under MACRS, the classes of property have changed as have the methods of computing depreciation. But other than that, there's hardly a difference!!

The major change, intended to enhance revenue collection, was to limit depreciation to the straight line method computed over 27.5 years for a residential rental property and 31.5 years for other real property. MACRS allows depreciation to be computed on a straight line basis over longer recovery periods than under the regular MACRS accelerated method. The percentage of depreciation for property placed in service after 1986 under the MACRS method for various classifications of property is as follows:

Table 6.2

Three-Year Property

Year	Half-year convention	Mid-quarter convention			
		First quarter	Second quarter	Third quarter	Fourth quarter
1	33.33%	58.33%	41.67%	25.00%	8.33%
2	44.45	27.78	38.89	50.00	61.11
3	14.81	12.33	14.13	16.67	20.37
4	7.41	1.56	5.31	8.33	10.19

advantageous method is listed below. Straight line depreciation can always be used.

Asset	New	Used
Personal property	200% D. B.	150% D. B.
Real property:		
Residential	200% D. B.	125% D. B.
Other	150% D. B.	S. L.

Prior to 1981, there was a special depreciation system known as the ADR System. It was essentially used by large corporations with substantial investments in depreciable assets. The ADR system was generally not used for small business.

[2] Depreciation Rules 1981-1986.

The federal government enacted substantial new depreciation rules for property placed in service in 1981. The California rules essentially remained the same through 1986. The new federal rules were called ACRS. Under the ACRS system,

Five-Year Property

Table 6.3

| Year | Half-year convention | Mid-quarter convention | | | |
		First quarter	Second quarter	Third quarter	Fourth quarter
1	20.00%	35.00%	25.00%	15.00%	5.00%
2	32.00	26.00	30.00	34.00	38.00
3	19.20	15.60	18.00	20.40	22.80
4	11.52	11.01	11.37	12.24	13.68
5	11.52	11.01	11.37	11.30	10.94
6	5.76	1.38	4.26	7.06	9.58

Seven-Year Property

Table 6.4

| Year | Half-year convention | Mid-quarter convention | | | |
		First quarter	Second quarter	Third quarter	Fourth quarter
1	14.29%	25.01%	17.86%	10.72%	3.57%
2	24.50	21.43	23.48	25.52	27.56
3	17.49	15.31	16.77	18.22	19.68
4	12.50	10.93	11.97	13.02	14.06
5	8.92	8.74	8.87	9.29	10.04
6	8.92	8.74	8.87	8.85	8.73
7	8.92	8.74	8.87	8.85	8.73
8	4.46	1.10	3.31	5.53	7.63

Three-year property generally consists of over-the-road tractors, special handling devices for the manufacturing of food and beverages, various farm animals, and other esoteric types of property.

Five-year property generally consists of cars, light general purpose trucks, and various types of equipment. Most property falls in the five-year class of property. Seven-year property consists primarily of office furniture.

---

assets were determined to be three-year property, five-year property, ten-year property or 15-year real property. Tables were then used to compute the depreciation based on whether the property was three-year property, etc. Between 1981 and 1986 the laws changed with repect to real property. 15-year real property became 18-year real property if it was placed in service after March 15, 1984, and before May 9, 1985. Real property placed in service on or after May 9, 1985, and before January 1, 1987, became 19-year real property. Depreciation computed using percentages designated in tables for the various classes of property (three-year, five-year, etc.) was computed on an accelerated basis. That is, the deprecia-

Ten-year property is depreciated using the 200% declining method. Fifteen- and 20-year property must use a 150% declining balance method.

Example

Depreciation of ten-year property placed in service in 1990 by Big Corporation would be determined as follows:

1   Divide the cost of the property by the number of years in the recovery period — 10 in this case.

2   Multiply the amount in (1) by 2 to reflect the 200% declining balance method.

3   Divide the result in (2) by two (The number "2" this time. Do you find this exercise to be overly cumbersome, or just plain wasteful of valuable productive time?) to reflect a half-year convention for the year the property is placed in service.

Depreciation in the second year would be determined by multiplying the cost of the ten-year property reduced by prior depreciation times 20%. Twenty percent reflects the double declining balance for ten-year property.

As you can see from the example, when property is placed in service during the year, it is assumed that it is placed in service midway during the year.

Important

A full year's depreciation is not available in the year property is placed in service.

A mid-quarter convention is used rather than mid-year if the basis of property placed in service during the last three months of the tax year is more than 40% of the property placed in service during the year, excluding real property. 27.5-year and 31.5-year real property uses a mid-month convention; i.e., the rules assume the

---

tion was in excess of the straight line method. The depreciation or recovery percentages of the various classes of property are as follows for property placed in service after 1980 and before 1987.

Three-Year Property		Five-Year Property	
Year	**Percentages**	**Year**	**Percentages**
Year 1	25%	Year 1	15%
Year 2	38%	Year 2	22%
Year 3	37%	Year 3	21%
		Year 4	21%
		Year 5	21%

Ten-Year Property			
Year	**Percentages**	**Year**	**Percentages**
Year 1	8%	Year 6	10%
Year 2	14%	Year 7	9%
Year 3	12%	Year 8	9%
Year 4	10%	Year 9	9%
Year 5	10%	Year 10	9%

property was placed in service in the middle of the month. Depreciation in subsequent years is computed by multiplying the rate by the cost of the property, reduced by prior depreciation, or by using the percentage in the tables for the various classifications of property.

Depreciation for property placed in service after 1986 is the same for California, for example, and federal with one notable exception. For California purposes, depreciation for corporate tax purposes remains the same as it was before 1987. The federal MACRS system only applies in California for individual income taxpayers.

Important

Not to confuse taxpayers or their advisers, but the ACRS (pre-1986 depreciation rules) and the MACRS rules will apply in California for residential rental property for which construction was commenced on or after July 1, 1985, and before July 1, 1988.

Depreciation, although a simple concept in real life, is complicated for tax purposes because the tax authorities have continually changed the rules. The purpose of this explanation is not to make the reader an expert on depreciation but to present in a very brief format the rules pertaining to depreciation. At least one legal publisher has published a two-volume explanation of the depreciation rules.

For federal purposes and in many states, such as, California, a taxpayer is allowed to expense up to $10,000 annually of certain business assets placed in service after 1986. For every dollar of investment in depreciable assets for the year over $200,000, the $10,000 amount is reduced by one dollar. Now that you have THAT clear...

Amortization is the recovery of the cost of an intangible asset using a straight-line method over the life of the asset. (Aren't you glad we explained that?)

15-Year Real Property

The applicable percentage is (use the column representing the month in the first year the property is placed in service.)

If the recovery year is	1	2	3	4	5	6	7	8	9	10	11	12
1	12	11	10	9	8	7	6	5	4	3	2	1
2	10	10	11	11	11	11	11	11	11	11	11	12
3	9	9	9	9	10	10	10	10	10	10	10	10
4	8	8	8	8	8	8	9	9	9	9	9	9
5	7	7	7	7	7	7	8	8	8	8	8	8
6	6	6	6	6	7	7	7	7	7	7	7	7
7	6	6	6	6	6	6	6	6	6	6	6	6
8	6	6	6	6	6	6	5	6	6	6	6	6
9	6	6	6	6	5	6	5	5	5	6	6	6
10	5	6	5	6	5	5	5	5	5	5	6	5
11	5	5	5	5	5	5	5	5	5	5	5	5
12	5	5	5	5	5	5	5	5	5	5	5	5
13	5	5	5	5	5	5	5	5	5	5	5	5
14	5	5	5	5	5	5	5	5	5	5	5	5
15	5	5	5	5	5	5	5	5	5	5	5	5
16	-	-	1	1	2	2	3	3	4	4	4	5

Important

Organization expenses of a corporation and of a partnership must be amortized over a 60-month period. Business start up expenses must be amortized over a 60-month period beginning in the month in which the active conduct of business begins.

Start-up expenses are amounts paid for creating or developing an active trade or business or investigating the creation or acquisition of an active trade or business.

Points to Remember

1   The computation of depreciation is rather simple except when you must do it for tax purposes.

2   Virtually constant changes make depreciation complicated.

3   After 1986, the California rules were essentially the same as federal for businesses conducted by individuals but substantially different for businesses conducted in the corporate form.

Repairs

The cost of repairing property is deductible if the expenditures neither materially increase the value of the property used in the business nor appreciably prolong its life. In other words, the repairs must simply keep the property in ordinary efficient operating condition to qualify. If the repairs materially increase the property's value or prolong its life, the repairs must be capitalized and recovered over time under the applicable depreciation rules.

The costs of carpets, refrigerators, a new roof, and things of that nature are capital expenses rather than repairs. An important consideration in determining whether an expenditure is deductible or should be amortized is the amount of the expenditures. A substantial increase in expenditures relative to prior years often means that

---

18-Year Real Property

The applicable percentage is (use the column representing the month in the first year the property is placed in service.)

If the recovery year is 1	2	3	4	5	6	7	8	9	10	11	12
1 9	9	8	7	6	5	4	4	3	2	1	0.4
2 9	9	9	9	9	9	9	9	9	10	10	10.0
3 8	8	8	8	8	8	8	8	9	9	9	9.0
4 7	7	7	7	7	8	8	8	8	8	8	8.0
5 7	7	7	7	7	7	7	7	7	7	7	7.0
6 6	6	6	6	6	6	6	6	6	6	6	6.0
7 5	5	5	5	6	6	6	6	6	6	6	6.0
8 5	5	5	5	5	5	5	5	5	5	5	5.0
9 5	5	5	5	5	5	5	5	5	5	5	5.0
10 5	5	5	5	5	5	5	5	5	5	5	5.0
11 5	5	5	5	5	5	5	5	5	5	5	5.0
12 5	5	5	5	5	5	5	5	5	5	5	5.0
13 4	4	4	5	4	4	5	4	4	5	5	5.0
14 4	4	4	4	4	4	4	4	4	4	4	4.0
15 4	4	4	4	4	4	4	4	4	4	4	4.0
16 4	4	4	4	4	4	4	4	4	4	4	4.0
17 4	4	4	4	4	4	4	4	4	4	4	4.0
18 4	3	4	4	4	4	4	4	4	4	4	4.0
19 ......-	1	1	1	2	2	2	3	3	3	3	3.6

the expenditures are not repairs. At any rate, such circumstances may very well draw an IRS review.

Points to Remember

1 The cost of repairs that do not materially increase the value of property or prolong the life of the property are deductible in the tax year they are incurred.

2 The cost of repairs that increase the value or prolong life must be capitalized and deducted according to a depreciation schedule.

Car expenses are common to almost all businesses. Unfortunately, the tax consequences of using a car in a trade or business are very complicated and frequently misunderstood. Major issues pertaining to business use of a car that concern most businesspeople are:

Car Expenses

1 Should the car be owned by the business or by the employee/owner of the business?
2 What deductions are allowed to employers for cars owned by them and used by employees who are less than 5% owners of the business?
3 What deductions are allowed to employers for cars owned by them and used by a 5%-or-more owner of the business?
4 What income is generated for employees who use a company owned car?

Many advisers suggest that cars purchased by a 100% owner of a business should be purchased by the business even if the car is not to be used 100% in the trade or business by the employee/owner. We disagree.

Owner/employees should purchase cars to be used in the trade or business in their individual capacity. The business, particularly if it is a corporation, should not purchase the automobile.

Tax Tip

In most cases, it is better for you, rather than your own company, to buy the car because if the car is not used 100% in the business, you

---

19-Year Real Property

If the recovery year is	1	2	3	4	5	6	7	8	9	10	11	12
The applicable percentage is (use the column representing the month in the first year the property is placed in service.)												
1	8.8	8.1	7.3	6.5	5.8	5.0	4.2	3.5	2.7	1.9	1.1	0.4
2	8.4	8.5	8.5	8.6	8.7	8.8	8.8	8.9	9.0	9.0	9.1	9.2
3	7.6	7.7	7.7	7.8	7.9	7.9	8.0	8.1	8.1	8.2	8.3	8.3
4	6.9	7.0	7.0	7.1	7.1	7.2	7.3	7.3	7.4	7.4	7.5	7.6
5	6.3	6.3	6.4	6.4	6.5	6.5	6.6	6.6	6.7	6.8	6.8	6.9
6	5.7	5.7	5.8	5.9	5.9	5.9	6.0	6.0	6.1	6.1	6.2	6.2
7	5.2	5.2	5.3	5.3	5.3	5.4	5.4	5.5	5.5	5.6	5.6	5.6
8	4.7	4.7	4.8	4.8	4.8	4.9	4.9	5.0	5.0	5.1	5.1	5.1
9	4.2	4.3	4.3	4.4	4.4	4.5	4.5	4.5	4.5	4.6	4.6	4.7
10-19	4.2	4.2	4.2	4.2	4.2	4.2	4.2	4.2	4.2	4.2	4.2	4.2
20	0.2	0.5	0.9	1.2	1.6	1.9	2.3	2.6	3.0	3.3	3.7	4.0

As indicated above, the depreciation percentages used in the schedule result in depreciation in excess of straight line depreciation. Taxpayers could elect to use the straight-line method of depreciation for the various classes of property and may have to reimburse your company (employer) or recognize income for the personal use of the vehicle. This recognition of income can continue for a substantial number of years if the car is expensive or a "luxury" car. The income recognition could even add up to more than the cost of the car — creating "phantom income."

Example

The Rich Corporation buys a $100,000 automobile. (That deal on a Rolls Royce was too good to pass up!) Mr. Rich, the 100% shareholder uses the car part of the time for personal purposes. Mr. Rich must reimburse the company for the fair market value of the personal use of the car or must recognize as income the fair market value of personal use of the car.

This income recognition could continue indefinitely. The income recognition over time could even be more than the cost of the car!

However, if the automobile were owned by Mr. Rich, he would not have to recognize income or reimburse the corporation for the personal use of the automobile. The corporation could reimburse the owner/employee for the business portion of use.

Also, any employee reimbursement of expenses, such as auto mileage, etc., should be made persuant to a requirement that the employee provide substantiation of the expenses to the employer. Otherwise the employee's deduction of such reimbursed expenses may be adversly affected.

Employer Owned Cars

If an employer buys a car for use by an employee, the employer can deduct the operating costs of the car and depreciation. The employer may treat the personal use of the car as a fringe benefit taxable to the employee. In such cases, the corporation could deduct 100% of the operating expenses and depreciation allowed on the car.

Example

McSales Company provides a company car to an employee who is not a owner of the business. The employee uses the car 75% of the time for business and 25% for personal use. The personal use is treated as a fringe benefit rather than having the employee reimburse the company for personal use.

The employer can deduct 100% of the operating expenses and the allowable depreciation for the year.

---

could elect to extend the recovery period — the period of time in which straight line depreciation could be taken. The following indicates the extended period over which property could be depreciated using the straight line method.

	Years
3-year property	3,5 or 12
5-year property	5,12 or 25
10-year property	10,25 or 35
15-year property	15,35 or 45
15-year property	15,35 or 45
18-year property	18,35 or 45
19-year property	19,35 or 45

If a car is used by a 5%-or-more owner of the company, the car **must** be used in the actual trade or business of the employer more than 50% of the time to be entitled to the maximum depreciation.

Caution

If an automobile is used less than 50% of the time in the business of the employer, treating the balance of the use as compensation to a 5%-or-more shareholder is not sufficient to be considered as being used 100% of the time in trade or business of the employer. If a car is not used more than 50% of the time in the trade or business, its depreciation must be computed using a straight-line method over 5 years. Depreciation cannot be computed using the 200% declining balance method.

The operating expenses attributable to the business use of the car may be deducted by the corporation. If the operating costs attributable to personal use are treated as compensation to the employee, they will also be deductible by the corporation.

If the car is used for personal purposes and then contributed to a business, depreciation will be the same way as if the car were purchased by the business except that depreciation is computed on the fair market value on the date the car is contributed to the business, if it is lower than the cost of the car.

Depreciation of automobiles depends on two factors:

1 Is it a luxury vehicle?
   (A car purchased after 1986 is a luxury car if the purchase price exceeds $12,763.)
2 When was it placed in service?

For cars placed in service after June 18, 1984, various luxury car rules apply.[3] The maximum deduction and Investment Tax Credit

---

If the straight line method was used for various recovery periods, the following schedule indicates the percentage of depreciation to be taken for the first year, the last year, and years in between the first and last year for other than real property.

Recovery Period	First Year	Annual Percentage	Last Year
3 Years	16.667	33.333	16.667
5 Years	10.000	20.000	10.000
10 Years	5.000	10.000	5.000
12 Years	4.167	8.333	4.170
15 Years	3.333	6.667	3.329
25 Years	2.000	4.000	2.000
35 Years	1.429	2.857	1.433
45 Years	1.111	2.222	1.121

Three-year property generally included cars and trucks and over-the-road tractors. Five-year property was generally defined as property that was not three-year property or ten-year property. Thus most personal property such as equipment used in the trade or business was defined as five-year property for depreciation purposes.

[3] There were no luxury automobile limitation rules for automobiles placed in service before July 1984. Depreciation was computed under the ACRS method for three-year property.

for luxury cars placed in service after June 19, 1984, and before 1987 is listed in table 6.5.

Automobiles used in a trade or business qualify under the $10,000 first-year expensing rules. Under the luxury car rules, the depreciation deduction and expensing deduction are combined for purposes of the maximum amount that is deductible. The maximum depreciation for cars placed in service after December 31, 1986 is as

Table 6.5

For Cars Placed in Service:	Depreciation MACRS post 1986 ACRS pre 1987	First-Year Expensing Election	Investment Tax Credit
After June 18, 1984, and before January 1, 1985	$4,000 maximum depreciation and first-year expensing deduction combined		$1,000 maximum credit, or
	$6,000 maximum deduction for each succeeding year in the period	No deduction for succeeding years	$666.67 maximum credit if reduced ITC is elected
After December 31, 1984, and before April 3, 1985	$4,100 maximum depreciation and first-year expensing deduction combined		$1,000 maximum credit, or
	$6,200 maximum deduction for each succeeding year in the period	No deduction for succeeding years	$666.67 maximum credit if reduced ITC is elected
After April 2, 1985, and before January 1, 1987	$3,200 maximum depreciation and first-year expensing deduction combined		$675 maximum credit, or
	$4,800 maximum deduction for each succeeding year in the period	No deduction for succeeding years	$450 maximum credit if reduced ITC is elected
After December 31, 1986	$2,560 maximum depreciation and first-year expensing deduction combined		No ITC allowed
	$4,100 maximum deduction for 2nd year	No deduction for succeeding years	
	$2,450 maximum deduction for 3rd year		
	$1,475 maximum deduction for each succeeding year in the period (including carryover years)		

follows. Cars (or other assets) placed in service after 1986 do not qualify for an investment tax credit.

Years Placed in Service	Amount or percentage
1	$2,560 or 20%
2	$4,100 or 32%
3	$2,450 or 19.2%
4	$1,475 or 11.52%
5	$1,475 or 11.52%
6	$1,475 or 5.76%
Subsequent years	$1,475 or 5.76%

The maximum depreciation is further limited to business use.   **Table 6.6**

Example

In 1988 John Big Bucks purchased a car for $18,000. He used it in his sole proprietorship 80% of the time during the year the car was placed in service and each year thereafter. Depreciation is computed under the regular MACRS method is as follows:

Year	Full Allowance	x	Business Use	=	Deduction
1988	$2,560		80%		$2,048
1989	$4,100		80%		$3,280
1990	$2,450		80%		$1,960
1991	$1,475		80%		$1,180
1992	$1,475		80%		$1,180
1993 and each year thereafter	$1,036		80%		$820

Depreciation in year seven and thereafter is limited to $1,475 or 5.76% of the depreciable basis of the vehicle, whichever is less (18,000 x .80 x 5.76 = 829).

Starting in 1989, the limitation on depreciation for luxury automobiles is indexed for inflation. The indexed limitations for automobiles first placed in service in 1989 are as follows:

Tax Year	Amount
First tax year (1989)	$2,660
Second tax year (1990)	4,200
Third tax year (1991)	2,550
Each succeeding year	1,475

Table 6.7

The value of the personal use of a vehicle provided by an employer is a taxable fringe benefit (see above). The employer must include the value of the fringe benefit in the employee's wages for income and employment tax purposes. If, however, an employee pays the employer for the personal use of the car, no income results.

If the value of the employee's personal use is very small and impractical to account for, such value need not be included in the employee's income. An example of this might be when an employee uses a car to drive to lunch or make an occasional side trip to shop.

Caution

The value that must be included in income for personal use is the fair market value of the use of the car in the same geographical area. If an expensive car is used 70% of the time in personal endeavors, the amount of the fringe benefits included as income may be substantial.

In certain cases, three alternative methods of valuing the personal use are available. These methods are the annual lease value method, the cents per mile method, and a commuter use value method. These alternative methods are really "safe harbors" that can be used, if an employee qualifies, to protect a taxpayer from the IRS asserting a greater amount of income.

Annual Lease Value Method

Under the annual lease value method, an amount is included in income based on the fair market value of the car when it was first available for personal use. The annual lease value is determined by using the table provided by the IRS and set forth below. The annual lease value indicated in the table provided by the IRS must be used for four years. At the beginning of the fifth year, the annual lease value must be determined based on the fair market value of the car as of January 1 of that year.

Table 6.7

Annual Lease Value Table

Automobile Fair Market Value	Annual Lease Value	Automobile Fair Market Value	Annual Lease Value
$0 to 999	$600	$22,000 to 22,999	$6,100
1,000 to 1,999	850	23,000 to 23,999	6,350
2,000 to 2,999	1,100	24,000 to 24,999	6,600
3,000 to 3,999	1,350	25,000 to 25,999	6,850
4,000 to 4,999	1,600	26,000 to 27,999	7,250
5,000 to 5,999	1,850	28,000 to 29,999	7,750
6,000 to 6,999	2,100	30,000 to 31,999	8,250
7,000 to 7,999	2,350	32,000 to 33,999	8,750
8,000 to 8,999	2,600	34,000 to 35,999	9,250
9,000 to 9,999	2,850	36,000 to 37,999	9,750
10,000 to 10,999	3,100	38,000 to 39,999	10,250
11,000 to 11,999	3,350	40,000 to 41,999	10,750
12,000 to 12,999	3,600	42,000 to 43,999	11,250
13,000 to 13,999	3,850	44,000 to 45,999	11,750
14,000 to 14,999	4,100	46,000 to 47,999	12,250
15,000 to 15,999	4,350	48,000 to 49,999	12,750
16,000 to 16,999	4,600	50,000 to 51,999	13,250
17,000 to 17,999	4,850	52,000 to 53,999	13,750
18,000 to 18,999	5,100	54,000 to 55,999	14,250
19,000 to 19,999	5,350	56,000 to 57,999	14,750
20,000 to 20,999	5,600	58,000 to 59,999	15,250
21,000 to 21,999	5,850		

For vehicles having a fair market value in excess of $59,999, the annual lease value is equal to: (.25 x the fair market value of the car) + $500.

Starting for 1989, the IRS will issue new tables for annual lease values for property placed in service during the year. The tables will be revised annually and indexed for inflation.

Cents Per Mile Method

If an employer provides a car to an employee and it is reasonably expected that the car will be regularly used in the employer's business or that the car will be driven primarily by the employee for at least 10,000 miles in a year, the value of the personal use may be calculated by multiplying the number of miles driven for personal use by the cents per mile rate. The cents per mile rate is 26 cents in 1990.

The cents per mile method may not be used if the value of the car exceeds the maximum recovery deductions allowable for the first three years under the luxury car limitations — to $12,060 in 1987 and subsequent years.

Caution

Commuter Use Value Method

Under the commuter use value method, an employee must include in income $1.50 per one-way commute. The commuter use value can be used if (1) there is a bona fide reason for the employee to use the car to commute, (2) the employer has established a written policy that the employee may not use the vehicle for personal purposes other than commuting and an insubstantial amount of personal use, (3) the employee actually does not use the car for personal purposes other than commuting, and (4) the employee required to use the vehicle is not an owner or officer of the business.

Surprising tax rules exist for employees who lease cars. The general rule is that the business percent of the cost of leasing the car can be deducted each year. To prevent individuals from avoiding the luxury car depreciation limits, the tax authorities have issued rules requiring that the lessee of the car recognize a certain amount of income attributable to the lease. The theory is that the deduction attributable to leasing the car is reduced by the amount of income recognized so that the net tax deduction is not more than would be allowed for depreciating the car under the luxury car rules.

Leased Car

The computation of the lease amount is rather complicated. The amount included in income is based upon the cost of the car. This income-recognition rule only applies to the lease of the car that has a fair market value in excess of $11,250, if leased after April 2, 1985 ($16,500 if leased after June 18, 1984 and before April 3, 1985).

The lease inclusion is computed by using tables provided by the IRS for cars of a certain fair market value multiplied by the percentage of business use. A sample of the table for a car with a fair market value between the $25,000-40,000 range is set forth below. An additional amount of income is recognized for cars leased before 1987 if the business use of the vehicle falls below 50%.

Table 6.8   **Lease Inclusion Table**

Fair Market Value Year of Lease

But Not Greater Than	Greater Than	Year of Lease				Fifth and Later
		First	Second	Third	Fourth	
$25,000	$26,000	$177	$386	$ 572	$ 686	$ 792
26,000	27,000	190	416	617	740	854
27,000	28,000	204	447	662	794	917
28,000	29,000	218	477	707	848	979
29,000	30,000	232	507	752	902	1,041
30,000	31,000	246	538	797	956	1,104
31,000	32,000	260	568	842	1,010	1,166
32,000	33,000	274	599	887	1,064	1,228
33,000	34,000	288	629	933	1,118	1,291
34,000	35,000	302	659	978	1,172	1,353
35,000	36,000	316	690	1,023	1,226	1,415
36,000	37,000	329	720	1,068	1,280	1,478
37,000	38,000	343	751	1,113	1,334	1,540
38,000	39,000	357	781	1,158	1,388	1,602
39,000	40,000	371	811	1,203	1,442	1,665
40,000	41,000	385	842	1,248	1,496	1,727

Example

On July 1, 1990 Joe Flo leased a sports car with a fair market value of $32,500. It is a 3-year lease with an annual lease payment of $8,900. The vehicle is used 80% for business during the 3-year period. The computation of the deduction and the amount included in income is as follows:

Year	Amount From Table 1	Proration	Busines Use	Income	Deduction	Net Deduction
1987	$274	184 : 365	80%	$110	$3,589	$3,479
1988	599	366 : 366	80	479	7,120	6,641
1989	887	365 : 365	80	710	7,120	6,410

Table 6.9

From the example, it appears that the deduction for the lease payment is in excess of the depreciation that would be allowed under the luxury car rules. Thus, there may be some benefits from leasing a car.

Tax laws are based upon the "substance" of transactions. Many automobile leases are, in fact, purchases of automobiles with a down payment at the end of the lease or finance period, rather than when the car is initially acquired. If a lease is a purchase, the car should be depreciated, and the lease payments cannot be deducted. A portion of the lease payments would be payment of principal on the deferred payment purchase, and a part of the payments would be interest expense.

Points to Remember

1   The tax consequences of using a car in a trade or business are very complicated.

2   An employer or employee can deduct the cost of operating a car in a trade or business.

3   Depreciation is limited if the car is a luxury car.

4   If an employee uses an employer's car for personal purposes, the employee must recognize income in the amount of the fair market value of the personal use of the vehicle.

5   If a car is leased, the percentage of the operating lease payments attributable to the business use of the vehicle is deductible. However, "phantom income" may have to be recognized. The tax authorities have prepared tables for use in leasing situations to ensure that the deductions are not substantially in excess of the amount of depreciation that would be allowable under the luxury car rules.

PALS & PIGS

One might have thought that the tax rules would go to the dogs but not to the pals and pigs! PALS and PIGS are acronyms for "passive activity losses" and "passive income generators." The Tax Reform Act of 1986 created these unique creatures.

Important

A passive activity loss (PAL) is a loss from an activity in which an individual does not materially participate on a regular, continuous, and substantial basis. The rental of real estate and tangible personal property is automatically considered a passive activity, even if the owner spends 40 hours a week tending to the rental of the property. In the true spirit of confusion, truly passive income such as interest is not passive activity income!

Caution

Losses from the rental of an apartment building or from any activity in which the taxpayer does not participate on a regular and continuous substantial basis can only be deducted against income from similar passive activities.

Income or loss from a limited partnership is deemed to be a passive activity giving rise to passive activity income or loss, even if the investor is a general partner in the same limited partnership. The passive activity loss limitation rules were rather drastic in the 1986 Tax Reform Act. They were retroactive in effect. Largely because of this, the legislation did allow a phase-in of the limitation. The following table shows the percentage of the net passive activity loss that can be deducted each year.

Table 6.10

Year	Percentage Deductible
1989	20%
1990	10%
1991	0%

The net passive activity loss that cannot be deducted against other income is suspended and carried forward to subsequent years until it can be used to offset passive activity income reported in such years.

"Active" and "Material" Participation

The material participation test can be met by either spouse. Material participation means regular, continuous, and substantial participation in the operations and/or management of a business. Simply approving plans for expansion, budgets, and so forth would not amount to material participation in management.

To meet the material participation test in management there must be a genuine exercise of independent expression and judgment. Everyday involvement is not necessary, however.

Note

There is an exception to the passive activity loss rules. Losses of up to $25,000 from the rental of real estate can be deducted against other income in certain situations.

In order to be able to deduct the $25,000, the taxpayer must actively participate in the operations of the rental real estate. Also, the taxpayer's adjusted gross income (AGI) must be less than $100,000 to deduct the entire $25,000. The $25,000 amount is phased out $1 for each $2 of AGI in excess of $100,000.

Bob Passive has an AGI of $125,000. He loses $25,000 from the rental of real estate. Only $12,500 of losses can be deducted against other (non-passive) income ($25,000 excess income divided by 2 = $12,500. That sum is subtracted from the $25,000 loss).

Example

Sue North's AGI is $150,000. She also loses $25,000 from real estate rentals. However, due to her higher income, none of the losses from the rental real estate can be deducted against other income. She can only use the $25,000 to offset passive activity income.

Example

The active participation test that must be met to deduct up to $25,000 of losses from the rental of real estate is less demanding than the material participation test to determine whether a activity is a passive activity or not. The active participation test is met if an individual makes bona fide decisions about accepting tenants, determining lease terms, and other related business matters.

You must have at least a 10% equity interest in the real estate and cannot own it as a limited partner to benefit from the $25,000 rental real estate exception.

Caution

If an activity is profitable, you may want to **fail** the material participant test. Then the profits of such passive activity could offset losses from other passive activities. These could include losses from limited partnership investments or from the ownership of real estate or equipment.

Tax Tip

If an activity is generating losses, you should become involved in the activity on a regular, continuous, and substantial basis. Then the losses can be deducted against other income.

Tax Tip

It doesn't matter how much involvement you have with respect to the rental of real estate, equipment, or other property because such activity is deemed a passive activity no matter what amount of participation.

If a business can be divided into two separate and distinct activities, it may be advisable to do so. The profits from one activity can offset other passive activity losses. The losses from the other activity may not be passive activity losses, if properly handled, and can be offset against any income. On the other hand, businesses may be combined so there is one activity that is not a passive activity.

Tax Tip

Ron Flier is a highly paid executive for Jettison Airlines. Mr. Flier purchased an office building and is a franchisee of a local retail outlet. The tax loss from the rental of the office building is $150,000. The franchise operation generates taxable income of $100,000. Neither Mr. Flier nor his spouse are involved in the day to day operations of the franchised store. Their main activi-

Example

Example cont.

ties are the original investment in the franchise, reviewing the monthly financial statements, and receiving the monthly positive cash flow.

Since neither Mr. Flier nor his wife materially participates in the franchise activity, the profits are passive activity income. They can offset the $150,000 loss from the rental of the office building. The rental of the office building is a passive activity no matter how much time, energy, and effort is put into the activity by the Fliers.

The determination of whether the franchise operation is passive or not is a function of the involvement in the operation by the Fliers. Since the operation is generating taxable income, it's better for Mr. and Mrs. Flier not to be involved on a regular, continuous, and substantial basis. Then the profits can offset other passive activity losses.

If the franchise operation generates a loss, Mr. Flier or his wife may want to get "materially" involved in the business so that it does not generate passive activity losses. The losses can then be used to offset Mr. Flier's substantial salary.

Corporate Passive Activity Rules

Closely held corporations (not electing to be treated as S Corporations) are not **completely** subject to the passive activity rules. A closely held corporation for this purpose is one in which more than 50% of the stock is owned directly or indirectly by five or fewer individuals. Professional service corporations — doctors, dentists, and other professionals — are not treated as closely held corporations for purposes of the exception and are thus subject to the PAL rules like an individual.

Important

Passive activity losses incurred by closely held corporations can be offset against any income earned by the corporation except portfolio income such as interest and dividends.

Tax Tip

In some instances where passive activity losses are generated, it may be advisable to have the passive activities conducted by a closely held corporation rather than by the individual owners of such corporations. In this way, the closely held corporation could use the passive losses to offset income from the business operations.

Profits or losses by an S Corporation are from passive activities or not based on whether the shareholder reporting the S Corporation profit or loss materially participates in the activity of the S corporation. A corporation that is not closely held as defined above is not subject to the passive activity law rules.

Important

A shareholder who materially participates in the activities of the S Corporation may deduct the losses (except from the rental of properties) against all income under the passive activity loss rules. Other tax rules, such as the basis rules or at-risk rules, may prevent the shareholder from using such losses, however.

Rental activities should still be owned by individuals and leased to their closely held regular (i.e., non-S) corporations. Rents should be high enough that the rental activity does not generate a loss. However, the rent cannot be unreasonable. If the rent is more than would be paid to an unrelated lessor, the rent, may be reclassified by the tax authorities as a dividend which is not deductible if paid by a regular corporation. Profits from leasing property to one's S Corporation or partnership will not be treated as passive activity income if the lessor materially participates in the operations of the S Corporation or partnership. Losses are still passive activity losses, however.

Tax Tip

1   The 1986 Tax Reform Act provides substantial new rules for passive and real estate investments. Losses from passive activities can only be deducted against income from similar passive activities.

Points to Remember

2   A passive activity is any activity in which the owner/taxpayer does not participate on a regular, continuous, and substantial basis.

3   The rental of real estate is deemed a passive activity no matter how much the owner/taxpayer participates in the real estate operations.

4   A taxpayer should not participate in an activity on a regular, continuous, and substantial basis if it generates a profit. Then such profits can offset losses from other passive activities.

5   If an activity generates a loss, the owner/taxpayer should attempt to participate on a regular, continuous, and substantial basis so that the loss will not be limited to offsetting only passive activity income.

6   Individuals can deduct up to $25,000 of losses from a rental real estate activity if they are actively involved in the business of renting real estate.

7   Closely held corporations other than S Corporations and personal service corporations can deduct passive activity losses against all income except portfolio income (usually interest and dividends).

As if the passive activity loss rules, etc. are not enough to confuse you or to prevent you from taking a loss, there are "at-risk" rules which say you cannot deduct certain losses from activities in which you are not at-risk. The rules, generally, apply to individuals and closely held businesses. They operate to prevent taxpayers from taking losses from real estate activities and other business or investment activities against salaries and passive income (and passive activity income) such as interest and dividends. A taxpayer will be at-risk if he/she has invested cash in an activity. The investment of cash (or other property owned by the taxpayer) puts the taxpayer at-risk — the tax payer can lose the cash, so the taxpayer is entitled to tax losses. A taxpayer is not at-risk with respect to

At-Risk Rules

amounts borrowed and used in an activity unless the taxpayer is personally liable to pay back the borrowed funds. Also, a taxpayer will not be at-risk if he/she is protected against losses because of guarantees or similar arrangements.

Prior to the 1986 change in our wonderful tax laws, investments in real estate were not subject to the at-risk rules. Losses from real estate acquired after 1986 (whether in partnership form or owned outright, etc.) are subject to the at-risk rules. Under special real estate at-risk rules, an owner will be deemed to be at-risk even though the real estate may be purchased with "loans" for which the owner is not personally liable (because the property secures the losn), but only if the loans are made by an entity in the business of lending money, i.e., a bank or similar organization.

Losses disallowed because of the at-risk rules are suspended and can be used when a taxpayer becomes at-risk.

Example:

Wanda Wonderful, a wealthy socialite, purchased a pig farm. She put $100,000 down and agreed to pay $400,000 over a four year period. The sales agreement provided that the $400,000 was not to be paid unless the pig farm generated cash flow during the four year period sufficient enough to pay the debt. Based on projections, there would not be cash flow to pay $400,000. Wanda is at-risk in the amount of the $100,000 paid down but is not at-risk for the $400,000. Thus, Wanda can only deduct up to $100,000 of losses because of the at-risk rules. As indicated above, the losses may be limited because of the passive activity loss rules, as well.

Points to Remember

1 If the taxpayer is not at-risk, the taxpayer may not be able to deduct certain losses until the taxpayer becomes at-risk.

2 The taxpayer is generally at-risk with respect to cash invested in an activity.

3 A taxpayer is not at-risk with respect to investments made with borrowed funds unless the taxpayer is personally liable to repay the borrowed funds. A taxpayer is not at-risk if he/she is guaranteed, etc., against losses.

CHAPTER

SEVEN

Measurement
and Timing
of Taxable Income

Measurement and Timing of Taxable Income

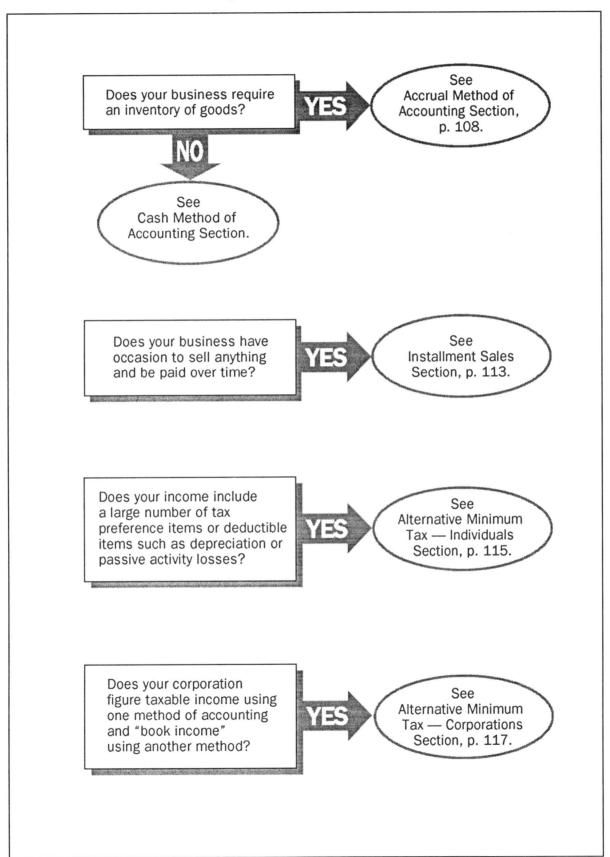

Does your business require an inventory of goods?

YES → See Accrual Method of Accounting Section, p. 108.

NO → See Cash Method of Accounting Section.

Does your business have occasion to sell anything and be paid over time?

YES → See Installment Sales Section, p. 113.

Does your income include a large number of tax preference items or deductible items such as depreciation or passive activity losses?

YES → See Alternative Minimum Tax — Individuals Section, p. 115.

Does your corporation figure taxable income using one method of accounting and "book income" using another method?

YES → See Alternative Minimum Tax — Corporations Section, p. 117.

This chapter deals with the methods of computing taxable income. In most cases, methods of accounting are the same for individuals, corporations, and partnerships. However, in certain instances, there are different requirements regarding the method of accounting depending on the form of a business.

Methods of accounting are the processes and procedures used to determine taxable income (or loss). There are essentially three methods of accounting. They are:

Methods of Accounting

1 Cash
2 Accrual
3 A combination of cash and accrual methods

In the cash method of accounting, income is recognized when cash is actually or constructively received. Expenses are recognized when they are actually paid. If you receive a check, cash, or other property in payment for goods or services, you are in "actual receipt" of income. Constructive receipt means that one has control over the receipt of the cash or other form of payment.

The Cash Method of Accounting

> Bill Checkwriter is a client of Jim Advisor. On December 30, 1989, he goes to see Jim. Bill has Jim's bill for $50,000 and carries with him a check which he plans to deliver. Jim tells Bill that it is better tax planning for his purposes if Bill would pay him on January 1 instead. Bill cordially agrees.
>
> However, in this case Jim has "constructively" received the payment of $50,000 because it was in his control to "take it or leave it."

Example

In the example, if Bill mailed a check on December 31 and Jim received it on January 2, the best tax results would be achieved by both parties. Jim, who is on the cash basis method of accounting (income is recognized only when it is received), did not actually or constructively receive income on or before December 31, 1989. Therefore he did not have income in that tax year. If Bill is also on a cash basis, he could deduct the expense in his calendar ending December 31, 1989.

Limitations on the Use of Cash Method

Not all taxpayers can use the cash basis method of accounting. A business that requires an inventory of goods must use the accrual method of accounting. In general, regular corporations (those that have not elected to be an S Corporation) and partnerships that have a regular corporation as a partner must use the accrual method of accounting.

Fortunately, for small business, the cash method of accounting may still be used by (1) taxpayers with average annual gross receipts of $5 million or less, (2) certain farming businesses, and (3) qualified personal service corporations. Qualified personal service corporations are corporations that perform professional services in such fields as health, law, engineering, architecture, accounting, and consulting. In these corporations, all of the stock is owned by the employees who perform the services.

The Accrual Method of Accounting

Under the accrual method of accounting, income and expenses are not reported when cash is paid or received but rather when the **rights** to the income and expense obligations take place. For a business that entails selling inventory, sales income may be reported for tax purposes:

1. when the goods are shipped,
2. when the product is delivered or accepted, or
3. when title passes to the customer.

Important

If a business requires an inventory of goods, it must use the accrual method of accounting at least with respect to that portion of the business that involves maintaining an inventory.

Under the accrual method, income is usually recognized when all the events have occurred which **fix** the right to receive such income and the amount can be **determined** with reasonable accuracy. As you may expect, deductions are accrued when all the events take place that determine the **fact** and the **amount** of liability with reasonable accuracy.

The time when income or expenses are accrued is basically the same — when it is known that it can be received or it has to be paid **and** the amount to be paid is known. Reasonable parties disagree occasionally regarding when an item can or should be accrued. There are other considerations. If the expenses are prepaid, they cannot be deducted if the accounting is on the cash or accrual basis.

Example

George is in the business of manufacturing and selling gadgets wholesale. Business is sensational. George decides to prepay three years' worth of accounting fees to his accountant, Xavier. If George is on the cash or the accrual method of accounting, he must capitalize the prepayment and take the deduction for the accounting fees over the three year period for which the payment relates.

Xavier, on the other hand, is on the accrual basis. Xavier recognized as income the prepaid amount even though it may not properly be accrued until a later time. [1]

---

[1] Bad Debt Reserve.

Prior to the 1986 Tax Reform Act, taxpayers using the accrual method of accounting could deduct bad debt expenses using a reserve method. They could estimate the amount of bad debts they would have on the sales for the year which were on the accrual basis. They could then deduct the estimated amount of bad debts.

However, the 1986 Tax Reform Act changed that procedure. Bad debts now can only be taken by specifically writing off the receivable that is deemed to be uncollectible. In other words, bad debts were deducted when it is determined that a specific debt will not be collected or will only be partially collected.

Points to Remember

1 A taxpayer's method of accounting is the procedure used to determine when income and expenses are recognized for tax purposes.

2 The cash and accrual methods are the two basic methods of accounting.

3 Under the cash method of accounting, income is recognized when actually or constructively received. Expenses are recognized when payments are made.

4 Under the cash method of accounting, expenditures must be capitalized if they relate to more than one period.

5 The cash method of accounting is generally the more flexible approach because receipt and payment can be controlled to a degree.

6 Under the accrual method of accounting, income and expenses are recognized when the right to the income or the obligation to make the expenditure takes place. This is generally when the fact of the right to receive or the obligation to pay arises and the amount can be reasonably determined.

7 Corporations other than S Corporations and partnerships with a regular corporation as a partner must use the accrual method of accounting. The major exception to this rule occurs when the corporation or partnership qualifies to use the cash method of accounting because it is a "small business."

8 A small business is generally one which has average annual gross receipts of $5 million or less for a period of time.

9 Businesses that have an inventory must use the accrual method of accounting.

Uniform Capitalization Rules

Accounting for inventories presents a whole different challenge. The 1986 Tax Reform Act established a uniform method for treating expenses incurred in creating an asset or holding an asset for resale. These uniform rules apply to manufacturing, retailing, wholesaling and to the construction of property whether for resale or use in the taxpayer's business.

The uniform capitalization rules require that all direct costs plus a proper share of indirect costs that are allocable to the property manufactured or held for sale be capitalized. Below is a list of the various expenses that must be capitalized in whole or in part or and those which may be expensed.

The uniform capitalization rules apply to both manufacturers and to retailers and wholesalers. Conceptually and practically, it is hard to apply such rules to retailers and wholesalers because they do not usually add value to a product. Nonetheless, the tax laws are designed to generate revenue and not necessarily to be fair, practical or economically accurate.

Table 7.1   **Uniform Capitalization Rules**

Expensed	Allocated & Capitalized	
	In Total	In Part
Direct Production Costs		
Material	X	
Labor	X	
Indirect Production Costs		
Repairs	X	
Maintenance	X	
Utilities	X	
Rent	X	
Indirect labor	X	
Production supervisory wages	X	
Indirect materials & supplies	X	
Small tools & equipment	X	
Quality control & inspection	X	
Marketing		X
Advertising		X
Selling		X
Other distribution expenses		X
Research & experiment costs under Section 174		X
Development & other costs under Section 263(c) & 616(a)		X
Section 165 losses		X
% depletion in excess of cost	X	
Tax depreciation & amortization in excess of financial depreciation	X	
Local & foreign income taxes		X
Past service costs of pensions	X	
Administrative (general)		X (1)
Officers' salaries (general)		X (1)
Taxes under Section 164 (other than local & foreign income taxes)	X	
Financial statement depreciation & cost depletion	X	
Employee benefits	X	
Rework labor, scrap & spoilage	X	
Direct administrative expenses	X	
Officers' salaries - direct	X	
Insurance sots - direct	X	
Cost of strikes		X
Bidding - successful	X	
Bidding - unsuccessful		X
Depreciation on idle property		X

(1) Allocate between deductible and capitalizable activities

Interest expense must be capitalized for construction of:

- Real estate.
- Property with a life of 20 years or more under the 1987 depreciation rules.
- Property with a construction period of two or more years.
- Property having a production period of more than one year and costing more than $1 million.

Fortunately, Congress was gracious enough to allow retailers and wholesalers to use a simplified method of allocating and capitalizing costs. Under the simplified method, off-site storage and warehousing, handling and processing, purchasing, and general administrative expenses are added to the purchase price of the property sold at wholesale or retail.

Caution

Accounting for inventory is a very complicated process for which a small business must receive the assistance of an accountant or CPA.

In addition to the rules as to what must be capitalized, there are further complicated rules on how to expense the capitalized costs. Once the capitalized costs are determined, they can be deducted as cost of goods sold using a first-in-first-out basis (FIFO) or last-in-first-out (LIFO) basis. Other methods exist, as well.

Under the FIFO method, the ending inventory and cost of sales reflect the position that older inventory is sold first. Under the LIFO method, the ending inventory and the cost of sales reflect the position that the last inventory manufactured, produced, or purchased is sold first.

Tax Tip

Usually during inflationary times, it's better to use the LIFO method of accounting. This is because the more recent higher costs of acquiring or producing property are allocated to the cost of goods sold rather than to the inventory not sold.

The following is a very basic example of computing the ending inventory and the cost of goods sold of a widget business using the FIFO method of accounting in an inflationary period (the costs of purchasing the widget raw materials are increasing). In the next example, inventory and cost of goods sales are computed on a LIFO basis.

Example

Widget Inc. has 50 units which cost $10 per unit of Widget inventory on hand at the beginning of the year. It purchased an additional 100 units during the year at a cost of $20 per unit. At the end of year it had 40 units in inventory. Using the FIFO method of accounting, the ending inventory is computed as follows:

Computation of Ending Inventory (FIFO Method)

	Units	Cost	Total Cost
Beginning Inventory	50	$10	$ 500
Purchases	100	$20	$2,000
Ending Inventory	40	$20	$ 800

Example Cont.

Using the FIFO method of accounting for inventory when there is less inventory on hand at the end of the year than was available at the beginning of the year, all of the ending inventory is attributable to inventory purchased during the year. Thus the cost per unit of inventory is $20 and the total cost is $800.

Computation of Cost of Goods Sold (FIFO Method)

	Units	$ Value
Beginning Units	50	$ 500
Purchases	100	$2,000
Total Available	150	$2,500
Less Ending Inventory	40	$ 800
Units & Cost of Sale	110	$1,700

The LIFO results are as follows:

Computation of Ending Inventory (LIFO Method)

	Units	Cost	Total Cost
Beginning Inventory	50	$10	$ 500
Purchases	100	$20	$2,000
Ending Inventory	40	$10	$ 400

Computation of Cost of Goods Sold (LIFO Method)

	Units	$ Value
Beginning Units	50	$ 500
Purchases	100	$2,000
Total Available	150	$2,500
Less Ending Inventory	40	$ 400
Units & Cost of Sale	110	$2,100

Obviously, the results are different for both the ending inventory on the balance sheet and the cost of sales expense. Using FIFO, the inventory on the balance sheet is more than for LIFO. On the other hand, the tax deduction (cost of sales) is greater when LIFO is used (assuming inflation causes costs of manufacturing to increase).

Needless to say, our example is an over simplification of the accounting for inventory and cost of goods sold.

There are "simplified LIFO rules" for small businesses. A taxpayer is a small business for purposes of this rule if its average annual gross receipts for the three preceding tax years did not exceed $5 million. Under the simplified method, inventories are to be grouped into pools of inventory in accordance with consumer price index detail reports or producer price indexes. Published indexes may then be used to determine the LIFO inventory values.

There are special rules (and as you might guess, they are complicated also) for accounting for long term contracts. One problem with such rules is that Congress constantly changes its mind. The 1986 Act provided one set of rules, the 1987, 1988 and 1989 Acts each further modified the rules.

Points to Remember

1   There are new uniform capitalization rules in which various direct and indirect expenses of producing goods must be capitalized as part of the cost of the goods produced.

2   There are simplified methods for allocating expenses to inventory for certain small retailers and wholesalers.

3   Not only are there complicated rules for determining what expenses are to be allocated to inventory but there are complex rules for determining what goods that have been acquired or produced in the year have been sold and what goods remain as inventory!

4   There are two major methods of computing the cost of goods sold: LIFO and FIFO. There are other methods as well.

5   The LIFO method is generally advantageous in an inflationary period. There are also simplified LIFO rules for small businesses.

Installment Sales

An installment sale is a sale in which a payment is received in a year other than the year of the sale. In 1986 the rules were modified. In 1987, 1988 and 1989 the rules were modified again, but California has not adopted all the revised federal rules.

Under the installment method of accounting, a pro rata amount of the profit is reported each time a payment is received. For example, if the profit on a sale is 50% of the sales price, each time a payment is received, 50% of the cash received is counted as profit and taxable income.

Under the current rules, if your business sells real property or tangible personal property in the ordinary course of business, you cannot use the installment method. Sales of certain types of farm property, time share units, and residential lots may be reported on the installment basis.

The sale of non-farm real property that is used in a taxpayer's trade or business or that is held for the production of rental income may be reported on the installment basis.

Caution

If the face amount of deferred payments from the sale of rental property exceeds $5 million at year end, there is an interest charge on the deferred tax attributable to the deferred payment obligations. In figuring the $5 million amount, only those individual sales of over $150,000 are counted.

The sale of rental real property for less than $150,000 can use the installment basis and is not subject to the interest charge.

State Installment Sale Rules

California, for example, has different rules for installment sales, etc. because it has not adopted all the federal rules inacted in 1987, 1988, and 1989.

If you sell real and personal property in the ordinary course of business ("dealers"), you may use the installment sale method. However, if you have borrowed substantial funds, some of the gain that would have been deferred under the installment method may have to be recognized. The gain that is deferred under the installment sales rules is a tax preference item for California alternative minimum tax purposes.

Points to Remember

1 An installment sale is any sale for which payment is received in other than the year in which the sale is made.

2 The profit from installment sales may be reported on the "installment method."

3 The pro rata amount of profit is allocated to each cash installment received.

4 Profits from the sale of real property and personal property in the ordinary course of business cannot be reported on the installment method.

5 The sale of real property used in the taxpayer's trade or business (such as an office building) can be reported on the installment basis.

6 In certain situations, interest attributable to deferred taxes as a result of using the installment method may have to be paid to the IRS.

7 There are still substantial differences between California and federal rules regarding installment sales. Check with your tax advisor before undertaking installment sale transactions.

Tax Years

The Tax Reform Act of 1986 required that all partnerships, personal service corporations, and S Corporations conform their tax years to the tax years of their owners. The rule applies to new and existing entities.

Partnerships, Personal Service Corporations, and S Corporations

These entities must adopt or change to a calendar year. There was one major exception to the tax year conformity requirement. You may have a noncalendar tax year if there is a business purpose for doing so. Also, due to heavy pressure from small businesses, entities can, within limits (see CAUTION on deposits), elect to adopt, retain, or change to a fiscal year.

Caution

If partnerships or S Corporations elect other than a calendar year tax year, they must make deposits with the government. The purpose of the deposit is to take away the value of tax deferral that is attained by owners of entities that elect to use other than a calendar year.

Personal service corporations are limited in the deductions that can be taken for amounts paid to owner/employees unless certain minimum amounts are paid to the owner/employees during the portion of the tax year ending on December 31.

A partnership, S Corporation, or personal service corporation may establish a business purpose if it has a natural business year for its particular trade or business. If a business has a non-peak period and a peak period, its natural business year usually ends shortly after the close of the peak period.

The business purpose test for having a noncalendar tax year is deemed met if for three consecutive years the taxpayer has received 25% of its gross receipts during the last two months of the fiscal year.

Important

Generally, the taxpayer must obtain permission from the IRS to use other than a calendar year. A new partnership, S Corporation, or personal service corporation may adopt a fiscal year ending in September, October or November. Form 8716 must be filed to elect other than a calendar year.

Caution

1 Partnerships, personal service corporations, and S Corporations must use the calendar year as a tax year unless it can be established that there is a good business reason to use other than a calendar year.

Points to Remember

2 If certain elections are made and penalty provisions followed, such entities can elect to have other than a calendar year, even if there is not a good business reason for such taxable year.

Under the alternative minimum tax system, individuals compute their alternative minimum tax and pay the greater of the regular or the alternative minimum tax. The purpose of the alternative minimum tax is to ensure that every individual with certain levels of income, more or less, pay some tax.

Alternative Minimum Tax — Individuals

The 1986 Tax Reform Act made significant changes in the alternative minimum tax (AMT). The AMT is based on your regular taxable income adjusted for certain deductions taken for regular tax purposes and increased by certain "preference items" that were excluded from income or provided phantom deductions.

The alternative minimum tax rate is 21%.

Important

Adjustments to the regular tax treatment of various items are explained below:

■ Depreciation of real property and tangible personal property is generally computed using a longer life and a method of depreciation that results in less depreciation. For example, real property placed in service after 1986 must be depreciated for alternative minimum tax purposes using a straight-line method of depreciation and over more years than for regular tax purposes.

■ Personal property placed in service after 1986 must be depreciated using a 150% declining balance method rather than 200% declining balance method.

■ Other adjustments are made for various kinds of deductions for businesses such as circulation expenditures for newspapers, mining exploration expenses for mining operations, and so forth.

■ The passive activity loss rules are being phased in for regular tax computations. However, for alternative minimum tax purposes there is no deduction for passive activity losses to the extent they exceed passive activity profits.

■ Significantly for most tax payers, no deduction is allowed for miscellaneous itemized deduction or state or local taxes.

■ Although the consumer interest deduction is being phased out for regular tax purposes, there is no deduction at all for alternative minimum tax purposes.

For alternative minimum tax purposes, certain benefits referred to as "preference items" are not allowed. Most of the preferences apply to unique benefits for certain types of activity such as percentage depletion for mining operations.

An individual can deduct the fair market value of certain property contributed to charity. For alternative minimum tax purposes, the amount of the deduction attributable to appreciation of the donated property must be added back to income.

Example

Carl Charming purchased stock in 1970 for $1 and contributed it to charity in 1989 when it was worth $10. Carl is entitled to a $10 deduction for regular tax purposes. However, for alternative minimum tax purposes he must add back $9 so that only $1 is deductible for alternative minimum tax purposes.

Since California has not conformed to the Revenue Act of 1987 as of early 1990, the deferred gain from installment sales is an adjustment to regular taxable income for California alternative minimum tax purposes though not for federal purposes.

As a result of changes made by the 1986 Tax Reform Act, the alternative minimum tax paid in prior years in certain cases will be a credit against the regular tax paid in a subsequent year. This credit can only be carried forward. The credit is all or part of the alternative minimum tax paid in a prior year. The computation of the credit carry-forward is very complicated. Essentially it allows for a credit against the regular tax when there was no regular tax benefit attributable to a deduction in a prior year. (You can see why we recommend that you consult a tax professional if you run into the AMT yourself.)[2]

---

[2] Prior to the 1986 Tax Reform Act, in essence either the regular tax or the alternate minimum tax was paid. There was no consideration in subsequent years whether the regular tax or alternative minimum tax was paid in prior years.

There is an exemption of $40,000 from alternative minimum taxable income. In other words, there is an additional deduction of $40,000 in arriving at alternative minimum taxable income. However, it is phased out when your alternative minimum taxable income exceeds $310,000.

The existence of the alternative minimum tax in many instances means that individuals are paying tax at a 21% rate. Before the 1986 Tax Reform Act, planning involved accelerating income and deferring expenses if one was subject to the alternative minimum tax. Subsequent to the 1986 Tax Reform Act, planning is much more complicated. In some instances, by accelerating income to the 21% rate, you are only prepaying your taxes.

The alternative minimum tax is one of the more complicated features of modern taxation. It proves that all the talk about simplification that accompanied the 1986 Tax Reform Act was misleading.

1   Individual taxpayers have to contend with computing regular tax and the alternative minimum tax.

2   The alternative minimum tax is based upon the taxable income for regular tax purposes with additions to income and deductions to arrive at an alternative minimum taxable income.

■   For alternative minimum tax purposes, a lower amount of depreciation is allowed each year.

3   The alternative minimum tax rate is 21%.

Points to Remember

Prior to the 1986 Tax Reform Act, corporations were subject to an add-on minimum tax. The tax was added to the regular tax computed on taxable income. The 1986 Tax Reform Act replaced the corporate minimum tax with the new and very complicated corporate alternative minimum tax, which is similar to the individual alternative minimum tax.

The corporate alternative minimum tax rate is 20%.

Like the individual alternative minimum tax, the corporate AMT is computed on alternative minimum taxable income reduced by an exemption. The exemption is $40,000 but is reduced by $1 for each dollar that alternative minimum taxable income is in excess of $150,000. There is no exemption once alternative minimum taxable income reaches $310,000. As in the case of an individual, part or all of the AMT paid by a corporation can be credited against regular tax in subsequent years.

The adjustments and preferences for purposes of the corporate alternative minimum tax are generally the same as for the individual alternative minimum tax. However, there is an additional adjustment known as the "book income" adjustment. If the taxable income is computed using one method, such as the cash method of

Alternative Minimum Tax — Corporation

Important

accounting, and the "book income" or financial statement income is computed using another method, such as the accrual method, one-half of the excess of the book income over the tax income is treated as an alternative minimum tax adjustment. This is a particularly significant adjustment for corporations that use the cash method of accounting for tax purposes but for purposes of securing loans, or for other reasons, use an accrual method.

For taxable years beginning after 1989 the preference is, generally, based on a corporation's earnings and profits rather than book income. Earnings and profits are generally based on cash receipts and cash disbursements.

Life insurance proceeds received by a corporation may be taxed because of this adjustment before and after 1989. It is book income but is not income for regular tax purposes. It is part of the adjustment for book income in excess of taxable income and therefore may wind up being at least partially taxable.

Example

Profit Corporation uses the cash method of accounting for tax purposes and reports zero taxable income after payment of compensation to employee/shareholders.

In order to secure a loan from a local financial institution, Profit Corporation prepares financial statements on an accrual basis which reflect income of $300,000 which includes $100,000 for receipt of life insurance on the death of one shareholder. One-half of the excess of the $300,000 financial statement income over the zero taxable income is treated as an alternative minimum tax adjustment. It is added to taxable income to arrive at alternative minimum taxable income.

Profit Corporation's alternative minimum taxable income is $150,000 reduced by the $40,000 exemption, or $110,000. The alternative minimum tax is $22,000 (20% X $110,000).

Points to Remember

1   There is an alternative minimum tax for corporations as well as individuals.

2   The preference items and adjustments for corporations are generally the same as for individuals.

3   There is a substantial additional preference item for corporate tax purposes. One-half of the excess of "book income" over "taxable income" is added back to regular taxable income. As a result, corporations which use the accrual method of accounting for book purposes and cash method for tax purposes may have to pay a substantial alternative minimum tax. The preference is based on earnings and profits rather than book income after 1989.

Capital Gains

The 1986 Tax Reform Act eliminated the preferential treatment of long term capital gains. Capital gains reported in 1988 and subsequent years are taxed at your regular ordinary income tax rates.

Capital losses can offset only $3,000 of an individual's ordinary income.   **Caution**

Capital losses are still fully deductible against capital gains. However, they can only offset $3,000 of an individual's ordinary income in any taxable year. Capital losses that exceed the total of capital gains and/or the $3,000 ordinary income can be carried forward for an unlimited period.

Capital losses of a corporation can be carried back three years to offset capital gains in those years. They can be carried forward for five years.

Capital losses cannot offset a corporation's ordinary income.   **Caution**

To determine what are capital gains or losses you need to know what is a capital asset. Tax law defines capital asset in terms of what is not a capital asset. A capital asset is any property but does not include the following:

- An asset held in the taxpayer's inventory.
- Property held primarily for sale to customers in the ordinary course of the taxpayer's trade or business.
- A note or receivable acquired in the ordinary course of a trade or business for services rendered or the sale of goods.
- Depreciable business property.
- Real property used in a taxpayer's trade or business.
- A copyright, literary, musical or artistic composition, or similar property (but not a patent or invention held by the taxpayer who created it).

Your personal effects such as an auto, residence, household furnishings, and stock investments are capital assets.

The definition of capital asset specifically excludes depreciable   **Important**
real estate or depreciable property used in a trade or business. However, if sales of such assets in any one year result in a combined gain, the gain is a capital gain. If the grouping of such sales results in a loss, the loss is an ordinary loss and not a capital loss.

Gains from the sale or exchange of capital assets are characterized as either short or long term depending on the length of time you held the asset. A gain or loss is long term if the property is held for more than six months, otherwise it is a short-term gain.

It does not matter whether the capital gain is long term or short term under present law since there is no favorable tax treatment for long term capital gains. However, there is a big difference whether it is ordinary or capital gain or loss. Capital losses can only offset capital gains and $3,000 of other income.

It is better from a tax standpoint to have an ordinary loss and a   **Important**
capital gain. Ordinary losses may be deducted against other ordinary income, and capital gains may serve to absorb capital losses incurred in the year or carried forward from prior years.

It is likely that in the future the law will change again to give capital gains preferential treatment. President Bush campaigned in 1988, 1989, and early 1990 for a cut in capital gains taxes.

Important

California and other states' capital gain and loss rules are the same as the federal rules except that the gain on the sale of residential rentals and certain farm property generates a tax credit in California.

Points to Remember

1   There is no longer a tax benefit from long-term capital gains.

2   Capital losses can only offset capital gains and $3,000 of an individual's ordinary income.

3   The amount of capital loss that cannot be deducted can be carried forward indefinitely for individuals.

4   Capital losses of a corporation can only offset capital gains. However they can be carried back three years and then carried forward five years.

Net Operating Losses

Net operating losses (NOL) are losses from the conduct of a trade or business incurred during the tax year. For federal purposes, net operating losses may be carried back by both individual and corporate taxpayers. To the extent the net operating loss has not been absorbed in the carryback years, it can be carried forward.

California now has partial conformity to the federal net operating loss rules. For California purposes, only one-half of the net operating loss may be carried forward and none may be carried back.

Under a transitional rule, for California purposes, 50% of the losses incurred in calendar years 1985 and 1986 may be carried forward to 1987, 1988, and 1989. Only a set percentage, an NOL, may be carried forward from income or tax years ending in 1985 (other than a calendar year). As per above, 50% of the loss can carry over for a year ending on December 31, 1985. The schedule below sets forth the percentage of a loss that may be carried forward for months ending in 1985:

Table 7.2

Income or taxable year ending	NOL Carryover
January 1985	4%
February 1985	8%
March 1985	2%
April 1985	17%
May 1985	21%
June 1985	25%
July 1985	29%
August 1985	33%
September 1985	37%
October 1985	42%
November 1985	46%
December 1985	50%

California law does not, at this time, permit carryovers of losses generated in income years beginning after December 31, 1991. For California purposes, the NOL carries forward for 15 years.

For federal purposes, an NOL can generally be carried back three
· years to the earliest year first and forward 15 years. A taxpayer may want to elect to forego the carryback and only carry the loss forward. Such an election may be valuable when the tax rate in the prior year was low and it is anticipated that the tax rate in the future years will be high.

Tax Tip

Blue Corporation has been in operation for several years. For its 1990 calendar year it incurs a $30,000 net operating loss. In each of its prior three years it had $10,000 of taxable income. It is anticipated that in the subsequent year it will have $400,000 of taxable income.

It is better for Blue Corporation to elect to forego the carryback of the net operating loss because the tax rate in each of the prior years was the lowest rate possible (because of the low taxable income). It will pay taxes at the maximum marginal rate in the succeeding year, assuming the corporation has the anticipated taxable income.

Example

Net operating loss incurred by individuals and corporations can be carried back for federal purposes. However, the operating loss for individuals must be computed using special rules. It is not merely the amount of the negative taxable income reported on the Form 1040 for the individual that can be carried back. For example, the negative taxable income is reduced by the personal exemption taken to arrive at the negative taxable income and the excess of nonbusiness-use itemized deductions over nonbusiness income, such as dividends, to arrive at the NOL carryback.

Caution

Points to Remember

1   For federal purposes, net operating losses from a business operated by an individual or corporation can be carried back three years or forward 15 years.

2   California only allows a carry **forward** of net operating losses.

3   California only allows one-half of the net operating loss to be carried forward.

4   Individuals' net operating losses are not merely the negative taxable income on their returns.

5   Adjustments must be made on an individual's return to compute the amount of the net operating loss that may be carried back and carried forward.

CHAPTER

EIGHT

Deferred
Compensation

Deferred Compensation

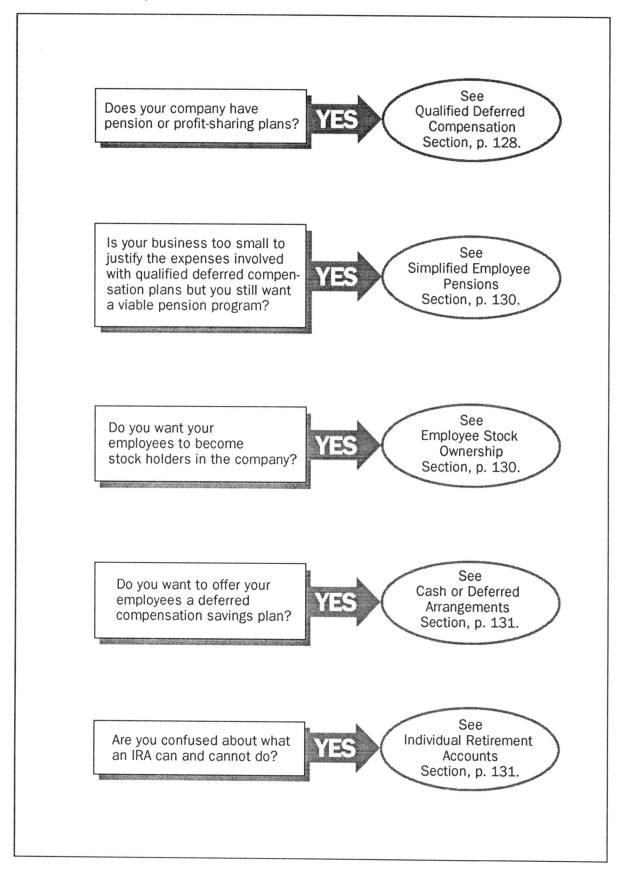

Does your company have pension or profit-sharing plans?

YES → See Qualified Deferred Compensation Section, p. 128.

Is your business too small to justify the expenses involved with qualified deferred compensation plans but you still want a viable pension program?

YES → See Simplified Employee Pensions Section, p. 130.

Do you want your employees to become stock holders in the company?

YES → See Employee Stock Ownership Section, p. 130.

Do you want to offer your employees a deferred compensation savings plan?

YES → See Cash or Deferred Arrangements Section, p. 131.

Are you confused about what an IRA can and cannot do?

YES → See Individual Retirement Accounts Section, p. 131.

There are two types of deferred compensation. One is a qualified deferred compensation plan such as a defined benefit or defined contribution plan. A defined benefit plan is a retirement plan in which deductible contributions are made to a trustee based on the compensation of the employees participating in the plan and their anticipated "pension" payments after retirement. A defined contribution plan is one in which deductible contributions are made to a plan trustee based on profits (and an employee's compensation) or some other performance measure. The other type of deferred compensation is termed "nonqualified" compensation plans.

The objective of deferred compensation for an employee is to defer the taxability of compensation. There is not usually a benefit for owner/employees of corporations or partnerships because the employer paying the deferred compensation is not entitled to a deduction until the compensation is paid. Deferred compensation is usually for non-owners of a business or individuals who may own a nominal amount of the business.

Nonqualified Deferred Compensation

Deferred compensation may take several forms. For example, the corporate employer may agree to pay a bonus based on performance of the company's stock, sales of a division, or some other measure for which the employee is responsible. The purpose of an employer paying such compensation is to provide incentive for employees to perform well and to stay with the company.

An important consideration for employees is whether the deferred compensation plan is "funded" or "unfunded." In an unfunded arrangement, the employer simply agrees to pay the employee a specified amount at a future date based on various criteria. The employee has no guarantee the amount will be paid if the company incurs financial hardship prior to or at the time the company is to make the payment.

The other approach would be to have the deferred compensation "funded." However, if the amounts funded are not forfeitable by the employee (i.e., the employee retains right to the funds even if he/she leaves the company), the funding will result in taxable income to the employee.

In fact, there is a rather prominent "catch-22" to the whole thing. For example, if a trust is formed and money is contributed to the trust to be held for future payment to the employee, the assets in the trust must be reachable by the creditors of the employer. If they are not, the employee has constructive receipt of the funds when they are contributed to the trust for his benefit. The employee will then have taxable income.

Important

In order for an employee to avoid taxable income with a "funded" deferred compensation plan, the deferred amounts must be subject to the creditors of the employer, resulting in risk to the employee that the amounts may never be received.

An employee can agree to defer receipt of certain compensation to a future date. The employee avoids taxation but also incurs some risk in that he is foregoing current payment of compensation for future payment. There is always a chance that the company will not be able to pay if it runs into financial difficulties.

Important

An employee's election to defer payment of compensation must be made before the compensation is earned.

Points to Remember

1   For an employee to defer compensation and the payment of tax on such compensation, the employee must not actually or constructively receive the compensation in the year it is earned.

2   An employee can agree with an employer to defer compensation to subsequent years as long as it is done before the compensation is earned.

3   An employee may be taxed on compensation that is paid in subsequent years if it is set aside for him in such a way that he is guaranteed of receiving the funds. For example, if compensation is placed in a trust that cannot be reached by the employer's creditors, the employee has constructive receipt. The employee would have to pay tax on the compensation.

4   An employer cannot deduct deferred compensation until such time as the employee recognizes it as income.

Qualified Deferred Compensation

Qualified plans generally consist of two types — a pension plan or a profit sharing plan, or both. There are more tax advantages to qualified plans: the contributions to the plans are deductible; employees do not have income until receipt of the funds; and finally, the income earned by the plans is not taxable at the "plan" level and is only taxed when paid out to employees.

A pension or "defined benefit" plan promises a specific amount of benefits payable in the future on a monthly basis to an employee based on (1) levels of compensation and (2) years of service. Contributions to the plan are actuarially determined so that the plan will be able to provide the promised benefits or amounts.

Contributions to a profit sharing plan, also known as a "defined contribution" plan, are usually based on profits. An employer generally is not required to make a contribution of a particular percentage to the plan. However, contributions must be (1) substantial **and** (2) recurring to continue the existence of a profit sharing plan. A profit sharing plan must have a definite written formula for allocating contributions to various participants in the plan. Contributions may be made to such a plan even though they exceed current and accumulated profits.

Various tests must be met for pension or profit sharing plans to qualify for the favorable tax benefits. The tests are essentially designed to prevent employers from discriminating in favor of owner employees. There are various complicated participation, coverage, vesting, and contribution requirements.

In addition, there are limits with respect to the benefits an employee may receive from a pension plan after retirement. The annual benefit for any participant may not exceed the lesser of $90,000 or 100% of the participant's average compensation for a three year period. The $90,000 figure is adjusted to reflect increases in cost of living.

The annual addition to a profit sharing plan for a participant's account may not exceed the lesser of 25% of the participant's compensation for the year or $30,000. The annual addition includes both the employer and employee's contributions and forfeitures of previous sums that were set aside for employees who quit the company before the benefits were completely vested.

Payment of benefits must usually begin at the earlier of two possibilities when the employee reaches age 65 or reaches normal retirement age for the plan. There are minimum distribution requirements with respect to qualified plans. There are stringent qualification requirements for "top-heavy plans," plans that primarily benefit an employer's key employees who are also the owners.

There are not any substantial differences between pension or profit sharing plans that are provided by self-employed individuals, corporations, or partnerships. In the early 1980s the laws were changed, resulting in general parity for all forms of business — sole proprietorships, corporations, and partnerships. Previously, the tax law favored qualified plans for corporations. Thus, many businesses were conducted in corporate form solely to obtain the greater tax benefits of qualified plans.

Points to Remember

1 Qualified deferred compensation plans provide substantial benefits for employers and employees.

   a Employers can contribute funds to a plan and deduct the amount contributed.
   b Employees do not recognize income until the amounts are distributed from the qualified plan in subsequent years.
   c The qualified plan is not taxed on the income it earns.

2 There are two types of qualified deferred compensation plans: pension or defined benefit and profit sharing or defined contribution.

3 With a pension plan an employee is guaranteed a certain amount at retirement. The amount contributed to the plan is a function of the employee's age, salary, and the guaranteed amount the employee is to receive during retirement.

4 With a profit sharing plan, certain amounts are contributed to the plan by the employer for the benefit of the employees. It does not guarantee an employee a certain amount at retirement.

5 For a small business to have a qualified deferred compensation plan, various tests must be met to insure that the employer is not discriminating in favor of the employee/owners of the business.

6 There are limits to the amount an employee can receive from a qualified pension plan upon retirement. There are also limits with respect to the amount of contributions to a profit sharing plan.

Simplified Employee Pensions — SEPs

In an attempt to make things easier for small businesses that may have difficulty justifying a qualified plan, Congress enacted legislation for Simplified Employee Pensions (SEP). A SEP is much less complex than a qualified plan. Employers who set up SEPs make contributions to an employee's IRA. Contributions to the IRA are not included in the employee's gross income.

The deductible amount that may be contributed to a SEP by an employer is the lesser of either 15% of the employee's compensation or $30,000. As with other qualified plans, there are non-discrimination rules to prevent the owner/employees from receiving most of the benefits under the SEP rules.

Contributions by a self-employed individual to a, SEP IRA set up after year end are deductible as long as the SEP IRA is set up and the contribution made by April 15 following the self-employed individual's calendar year end.

Points to Remember

1 Simplified employee pension plans are designed for small businesses.

2 SEPs allow an employer to contribute to an employee's IRA amounts in excess of what an employee could contribute to an IRA.

3 SEPs provide for limited administration hassles but have non-discrimination provisions similar to regular qualified plans.

4 SEP IRAs may be set up after year end.

Employee Stock Ownership - ESOPs

An employee stock ownership plan (ESOP) is a qualified deferred compensation plan designed to invest primarily in the employer's stock. Employees then have an ownership interest in their corporate employer. An ESOP is a form of profit sharing plan. The stock of the employer purchased by an ESOP is held in trust for the benefit of the participating employees. It is distributed to them in connection with their retirement or other termination of employment.

An ESOP provides an incentive for employees. They have more incentive to work harder and more efficiently because to do so will increase the value of the employer's stock and therefore the value of the employee's portion of the ESOP.

An ESOP also serves as a financing vehicle for the employer. Typically, this is done by having the ESOP borrow funds from a bank. The funds are to be repaid in five equal installments bearing an "arm's-length" rate of interest. The ESOP uses the loan proceeds to purchase stock in the employer corporation. The corporation guarantees the bank loan to the ESOP. The employer makes payments to the ESOP of amounts to cover the ESOP's principal and interest payment on the debt. The contributions by the corporation to the ESOP to pay the debt are tax deductible.

A principal advantage for employers with ESOPS is they can borrow funds and then repay the funds on a tax deductible basis. A truly unique feature!

Important

In addition to the ESOP benefits for employers and employees, commercial lenders exclude from income 50% of the interest income received on loans made to an ESOP. However for loans made after July 10, 1989 the exclusion applies only if the ESOP owns more than 50% of the corporate employer.

If the corporate employer pays dividends, a deduction is allowed for dividends paid to an ESOP. Another unique feature!

Important

There are substantial benefits for small business owners to form ESOPs. However, many small business owners have not taken advantage of the ESOP benefits because establishing and operating ESOPs are technical and the employees do become owners of the business.

1 An ESOP is a qualified plan which invests in an employer's stock.

Points to Remember

2 ESOPs are typically for larger businesses owned by individuals who do not wish to pass the business on to the family but prefer to sell it to corporate employees.

3 Typically, an ESOP borrows funds from a bank and uses the loan to purchase employer stock.

4 Payments to the ESOP to cover the principal and interest on the loan are deductible by the corporation.

5 Qualified lenders can in some situations exclude 50% of the interest income received from ESOPs.

Another qualified retirement planning device is the cash or deferred plan — commonly referred to as a 401(K) plan. Under a 401(K) plan employees can elect to have a set amount of compensation contributed to the plan rather than paid directly to them. Employees avoid taxation on the amount of the income that is contributed to the plan. The 1986 Tax Reform Act set a $7,000 limit in most cases on the amount that can be contributed to a plan. A 401(K) plan must meet strict non-discrimination requirements that prevent the owner/employees from receiving the majority of the benefits from the plan.

Cash or Deferred Arrangements — Section 401(K)

1 Under Section 401(K) plans, employees can exclude from immediate taxation compensation that is paid directly to the plan by the employer.

Points to Remember

2 Only $7,000 can be contributed annually to a 401(K) plan by an employee.

3 There are nondiscrimination rules that prevent employee/owners from taking undue advantage of 401(K) plans.

Individual Retirement Accounts — IRAs

IRAs have long been a tax-favored method of saving for retirement. One problem with IRAs is the rules keep changing. Of course, changing tax rules are not unique to IRAs! Currently, an individual who is not an active participant in an employer's retirement plan can make a tax deductible contribution of up to $2,000. However, if the individual is an active participant in an employer plan, the IRA deduction is limited based on the level of income and filing status. For a married couple filing a joint return, the income limitations are applied to both individuals. "Active participant" generally means any employee who is eligible to participate in an employer's qualified plan, even though he/she may not actually participate.

The ability to deduct an IRA contribution is phased out between $25,000 and $35,000 of adjusted gross income for a single taxpayer. For married couples filing a joint return, the phase out is between $40,000 and $50,000 of adjusted gross income.

The amount which can be contributed and deducted for a spousal IRA is $2,250. The spousal IRA may be beneficial when only one spouse has earned income.

It is important to be clear on the difference between what you can contribute and what can be deducted. Even with the most recent changes concerning IRA tax treatment, you can still contribute up to $2,000 per year, even if you are an "active participant" in your employer's plan. However, you cannot **deduct** your contribution.

What this means is that your IRA investment can still grow on a tax-deferred basis (the earnings are not taxed until money is actually withdrawn from the IRA). But that growth is on "after-tax" dollars. If you are not an active participant in an employer's plan, then your IRA becomes doubly valuable because you are working with pre-tax dollars since you get to deduct the amount contributed.

Example

Mary Jones and her husband, Frank, file a joint return for 1990. Mary's compensation was $30,000. Frank earned $20,000. Their adjusted gross income is $45,000. Mary is an active participant in her employer's qualified plan. $4,000 may be contributed by Mary and Frank to an IRA but only $2,000 can be deducted.

The amount that can be deducted is phased out for a married couple participating in a qualified plan when the adjusted gross income exceeds $40,000. The deduction is completely phased out when adjusted gross income exceeds $50,000.

In the example, one-half of the deduction is phased out at the $45,000 mark.

Following the promulgation of the new IRA rules after passage of the 1986 Tax Reform Act, many people mistakenly believed that there was no advantage to having an IRA if you did not qualify for the deduction. However, that is clearly wrong. The income earned in an IRA is not subject to tax until it is distributed. Your IRA can still accumulate earnings without paying any income tax.

Example

Ralph Anderson is married. He earns $100,000 a year as a salesperson for Big Sales Corporation. Big Sales has a qualified plan but Ralph cannot participate until 1991.

Mr. Anderson contributes $2,000 to an individual retirement account by the due date of the tax return for the 1990 calendar year. Mr. Anderson may deduct the entire $2,000 because he was not eligible to be an active participant in a qualified plan maintained by his employer, or Mr. Anderson may make a contribution to his spousal IRA of up to $2,250, even if the spouse does not have any earned income, and deduct such contribution.

Prior to 1987, there was no conformity between the federal and California IRA rules. The ability to deduct contributions to an IRA for California purposes were substantially limited. Before 1987 a California deduction was dependent upon whether the employee was a participant in a qualified plan. But there was no such limitation for federal purposes. The result was that deductions were quite often allowed for federal tax purposes but not for California tax purposes. Because of this difference, when amounts are actually distributed from an IRA to a recipient because of retirement, a different amount is taxable for federal than for California purposes. Since there was not a deduction in many instances for California purposes an amount can be excluded from California income equal to the nondeductible contributions.

Example

Sam Stallion was an employee of Jumbo Corporation from 1980 through 1986. He was a participant in the employer's qualified employee plan. He contributed $2,000 each year to an IRA and deducted such amounts for federal tax purposes but not for California tax purposes. In 1987 $20,000 was properly distributed from the IRA to Mr. Stallion.

For federal income tax purposes, Mr. Stallion would recognize $20,000 of income — the $12,000 that was contributed and deducted and $8,000 of earnings. However, for state tax purposes, Mr. Stallion would only include $8,000 in income because he did not deduct for California tax purposes the $12,000 contributed to the IRA.

Distributions from an IRA to a participant before the participant reaches age 59-1/2 are subject to a 10% penalty tax. However, the penalty does not apply for distributions that are a part of the series of substantial equal periodic payments over the life expectancy of the participant or joint lives of the participant and other beneficiary. This may be a beneficial form of distribution by an IRA if an individual retires early or simply needs cash flow for living expenses, etc. Distributions from an IRA must commence no later than April 1 following the calendar year in which the owner reaches age 70-1/2.

Points to Remember

1   Individuals can contribute up to the lesser of either $2,000 or the individual's earned income each year to an IRA.

2   If the individual or individual's spouse does not participate in a qualified plan, the contribution is fully deductible.

3   If the individual or individual's spouse participates in a qualified plan, the deduction for the $2,000 contribution to an IRA is phased out once adjusted gross income reaches $35,000 for a single taxpayer and $50,000 for a joint return.

4   Even though an IRA contribution may not be deductible, it still may be advantageous because the income earned in the IRA is not taxed until distributed to the IRA owner.

5   There were substantial differences between federal and California rules for deducting contributions to IRAs. As a result, distributions from IRAs in subsequent years are taxed differently for federal purposes than for California purposes.

6   There are rules pertaining to when distributions must be made by IRAs and penalties for certain early or premature distributions.

CHAPTER

NINE

_____

Corporate Tax Rules

Corporate Tax Rules

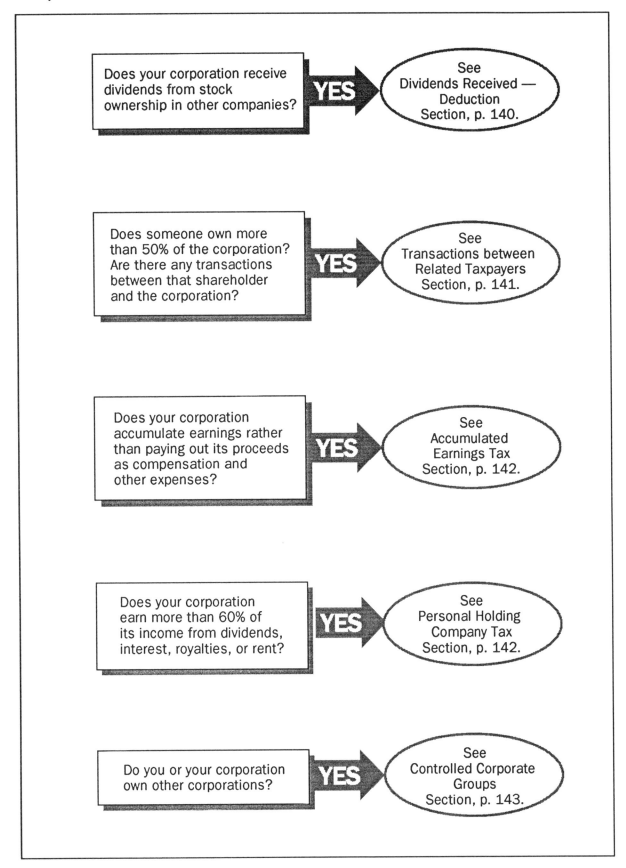

The general principles of income taxation apply to all taxpayers — individuals, estates, trusts, partnerships, and corporations. For the most part, there are no special rules with respect to the recognition of income, method of accounting, or depreciation method, whether the business is conducted as a sole proprietorship or corporation or partnership.

Exceptions do exist such as in California. For individual tax purposes, the California depreciation rules are the same as the federal rules for property placed in service after 1986. However, California retained its former depreciation rules for corporations.

There is a difference in the amount of depreciation and method of computing depreciation in California, depending on whether the business is conducted as a corporation or not.

Caution

In some cases there are special rules resulting from the relationship between a corporation or partnership and its shareholders or partners. For example, expenses payable to certain owners cannot be accrued by a partnership or corporation if the result is that the corporation or partnership gets a deduction in one year and the owner does not recognize income until a subsequent year.

There are, however, basic rules or issues that must be understood that pertain solely to conducting a business as a corporation.

The first issue is, what is a corporation? Another issue is, when will an entity be taxed as if it were a corporation? An entity will clearly be taxed as a corporation if it is properly incorporated.

Entities such as partnerships or trusts which have the characteristics of corporate limited liability are taxed as if they are corporations. This rule most often applies to limited partnerships. If properly planned and structured, a limited partnership will not be taxed as if it were a corporation.

Caution

1   The principles of income taxation are the same whether a business is conducted in corporate, partnership, or sole proprietor form.

Points to Remember

2   Exceptions exist such as California depreciation rules for corporations are different than the federal rules. California depreciation rules for corporations are different from the California rules for individuals.

3   An entity that has duly incorporated will be taxed as a corporation.

4   Some limited partnerships which are not properly and carefully organized and operated may wind up being taxed as if they were corporations.

Dividends Received — Deduction

For federal purposes, if a corporation receives dividends from other corporations, it is entitled to a "dividends received deduction." The deduction is 100% of the dividends received from a related corporation. For this purpose a related corporation is one in which 80% of the stock of the related corporation is owned directly or indirectly by the other corporation. If the 80% ownership test is not met, then the dividends received deduction is only equal to 80% of the dividends received.

There is a complicated hitch in that the aggregate amount of the dividends received deduction which may be taken by a corporation is limited to 80% of its taxable income computed without various items of income and expense including the dividends received deduction. However, this limitation does not apply if the deduction of the full 80% results in a net operating loss. This is a very esoteric and technical matter which can have an adverse impact.

The 1986 Tax Reform Act added a new provision called "extraordinary dividends." If a corporation receives an extraordinary dividend from another corporation, the recipient corporation may be required to reduce its basis in the stock of the dividend paying corporation. This basis reduction rule generally applies if the dividend that is received is more than 10% of the taxpayer's tax basis in the stock or fair market value of the stock of the dividend paying corporation.

Important

For California purposes, a corporation can exclude from income dividends paid by another corporation only if the paying corporation paid California income tax on its earnings. Also, California allows dividends received from a corporation included in a "combined" tax return to be excluded from income.

Points to Remember

1   On the federal level, a corporation is entitled to a deduction if it receives a dividend from another corporation.

   a   The deduction is 100% of the dividend received if it is from a related corporation.
   b   The deduction is 80% if it is not from a related corporation.

2   If an "extraordinary dividend" is received, there are provisions for reducing basis in the shares of stock of the dividend paying corporation.

3   California allows a deduction for dividends received by corporations only if the paying corporation paid California income taxes on its earnings.

4   In California, intercorporate dividends in a combined return are not taxable.

Organization and Start-up Expenses

Costs of incorporating, such as legal and accounting fees, must be capitalized by the corporation. If the corporation elects, it can amortize such expenses over a period of not less than 60 months beginning with the first month the corporation is actively conducting business. Start-up expenses incurred before business commences must be capitalized and amortized over a 60-month period, as well.

To qualify as an organization expense, expenses must be incurred before the end of the first tax year in which the corporation is conducting business. This may be a problem if the first tax year of the corporation is a short tax year.

Important

Zee Corporation was formed by its sole shareholder Xavier. Zee Corporation rented corporate office space. It reviewed opportunities to enter the fast food service business as a franchisee and other business opportunities.

Example

The rental expense is a business start-up expenditure incurred before any trade or business began. It must be capitalized and amortized over 60 months. Costs of acquiring a franchise or other business must be capitalized to the various assets acquired. These capitalization rules apply to all taxpayers, no matter what business form is used.

1   Organization and start-up expenses incurred by a corporation must be capitalized and amortized over a period of not less than 60 months.

Points to Remember

Expenses incurred by an accrual basis taxpayer cannot be deducted until actually paid if they are paid to certain related parties. This rule covers salaries, interest, rent, and other similar expenses. A related party is any individual who owns more than 50% of the corporation. Similar rules apply to losses between related parties. An S Corporation shareholder and an S Corporation as well as a partner and a partnership are related parties for purposes of this rule.

Transactions Between Related Taxpayers

Harry Figone is the sole shareholder of Manufacturing Inc. The corporation is on the accrual basis of accounting. It accrues a bonus on December 31, 1990 payable to Harry. The bonus is not paid until January 1991.

Example

Although the bonus can be properly accrued under the accrual method of accounting, it is not deductible until it is actually paid. If Harry had only owned 50% of the corporation, the bonus could be accrued by the corporation and deducted before it was actually paid.

1   A corporation cannot deduct an accrued expense to an individual who owns more than 50% of the corporation until such time as the expense is actually paid.

Points to Remember

Sale of Depreciable Assets Between Related Taxpayers

Since capital gains at this point in time no longer receive a tax preference, this is not as important an issue as it was in prior years. However, it still prevents a related party from creating a capital gain that can offset other capital losses.

Caution

Capital gain treatment will be denied in cases where depreciable property is sold to a related party. The purchasing party cannot receive an ordinary income tax deduction for depreciation while the selling party reports a capital gain.

Related parties for purposes of this issue are "controlled and controlling" entities. A controlled entity is a partnership or corporation in which a taxpayer owns directly or indirectly 50% or more of the stock or partnership interest.

Points to Remember

1   Gain from the sale of depreciable property among related parties must be reported as ordinary income rather than capital gain income. This prevents the purchaser from taking ordinary depreciation deductions when the selling related party reported capital gain income.

Accumulated Earnings Tax

In addition to the regular tax and alternative minimum tax, profitable corporations may have to pay a tax designed to penalize success — the accumulated earnings tax.

Caution

If a corporation accumulates its earnings rather than paying them out to shareholders as dividends, there is an onerous penalty tax that could be assessed.

Tax Tip

The accumulated earnings penalty tax is not usually levied against closely held corporations because the earnings should be paid to the owner/employees as salary, rents, interest on loans, and other expenses. If there is the danger that such payments would be disallowed by the IRS as unreasonable, the closely held corporation should consider electing to be treated as an S Corporation. S Corporations are not subject to the accumulated earnings tax.

Important

The accumulated earnings tax only applies if the earnings are accumulated for the purpose of preventing the imposition of an income tax upon the shareholders. A corporation may have a factual problem of convincing the IRS that this was not the purpose of the accumulation. Legitimate reasons to accumulate income would be to expand the business, to provide a surplus for contemplated repairs, and so on.

Caution

The corporate minutes should reflect legitimate reasons for the accumulation of earnings to prevent being penalized by the accumulate earnings tax.

The tax rate is a flat 28% and is imposed on accumulated taxable income for each tax year. The accumulated taxable income is essentially the taxable income reduced by taxes paid and dividends paid. A corporation may accumulate $250,000 without being subject to the accumulated earnings tax. The $250,000 amount is reduced to $150,000 for personal service corporations.

Personal Holding Company Tax

If a corporation is a personal holding company, it may have to pay a penalty tax of 28% on its undistributed personal holding company income. This onerous tax applies to corporations which have large amounts of passive income such as dividends and interest. A corporation is a personal holding company if 60% of its income is passive income, such as dividends, interest, royalties, or certain types of rent. To be subject to the personal holding company tax, five or fewer individuals must own more than 50% of the corporation.

An S Corporation is not subject to the personal holding tax.

1   Corporations may have to pay penalty taxes in the form of an accumulated earnings tax or personal holding company tax.

2   The accumulated earnings tax is paid if a corporation accumulates its income rather than paying it to its shareholders.

3   The accumulated earnings tax only applies if earnings are accumulated to prevent taxation of shareholders.

4   Corporate minutes must clearly reflect the reasons for any accumulation to avoid the penalty.

5   A corporation may accumulate $250,000 ($150,000 for a personal service corporation) without being subject to the tax.

6   The personal holding company tax may apply if a corporation has few owners and substantial passive income, such as interest and dividends, and the corporation does not distribute its income or pay dividends.

Important

Points to Remember

Various benefits that are available to corporations, such as the $250,000 exemption from the accumulated earnings tax and the benefit of the graduated income tax rates, must be allocated to all the corporations that are part of a controlled corporate group where the parent corporation owns 80% of the subsidiary corporations. A controlled group is a parent subsidiary relationship.

Brother/sister corporations (two corporations owned by the same individual) will be a controlled corporate group if 80% or more of the stock of the corporate entities is owned directly or indirectly by five or fewer individuals. The reason for this rule is to prevent the same owners from forming corporations to take advantage of various tax benefits such as the graduated rates. If it weren't for this rule, many corporations could be organized and operated so that the taxable income of each corporation is no more than the amount which would be subject to the lowest graduated tax rate.

Controlled
Corporate Groups

Joe Wheelerdealer owns and operates three corporations. He anticipates having net income of about $150,000 total for all three corporations from manufacturing soda pop. Joe must operate the business in corporate form to limit the liability from manufacture of the product. He wants to leave the $150,000 profits in the business to expand the business to meet the pent-up demand for his product.

Example

Example cont.

Each corporation reports taxable income of $50,000. The tax rate on the first $50,000 of a corporation's taxable income is 15%. However, because the three corporations are part of a controlled group, only one 15% rate bracket is allocated to the total $150,000 of taxable income earned by the three corporations. Thus, the total tax that would be paid on the $150,000 is:

Rate	Amount	Tax
15%	$ 50,000	$ 7,500
25%	25,000	6,250
34%	75,000	25,500
	$150,000	$39,250

The total tax paid by the controlled group is $39,250, rather than $22,500, if the three corporations only had to pay the 15% rate on their taxable income of $50,000.

Points to Remember

1   Controlled corporation group tax laws are designed to prevent abuse of certain tax benefits such as access to the lowest graduated tax rates by companies owned by the same people.

Consolidated Returns

If a parent corporation owns 80% or more of the stock of a subsidiary corporation, the two (or more) corporations may file a federal consolidated income tax return. One benefit of a consolidated tax return is that losses from one corporation can offset profits of another. If a consolidated return was not filed, the profitable corporation would have to pay income tax and could not benefit from the loss incurred by the other corporation.

States may not allow the filing of a consolidated return but does allow the filing of a combined return. A combined return may be filed when the same interests own more than 50% of the corporation's stock. The combined return rules apply to a parent subsidiary relationship where one corporation owns more than 50% of another corporation and to brother/sister situations where one individual owns 50% of the stock of two or more corporations. The filing of a combined return for brother/sister corporations is clearly unique to California. There is no similar federal rule.

Combined returns are authorized by state tax laws to prevent the tax evasion. State tax authorities may not allow the filing of a combined return in some situations. This usually comes up if the combined return is for a profitable corporation with a losing corporation.

Points to Remember

1   On the federal level, parent corporations which own more than 80% of subsidiary corporations can file consolidated returns.

2   One major benefit of filing a consolidated return is that losses in one corporation can be used to offset profits in another.

3   State generally do not have consolidated returns. In some cases the state allows filing combined returns for corporations more than 50% owned by the same interests.

4   State tax authorities may not allow filing combined returns which offset the profits of one company with the losses of another.

Corporate estimated tax requirements are similar to the requirements for individuals. The fourth estimate for corporate tax purposes is due on the 15th day of the 12th month of the tax year — that would be December 15 (rather than January 15 of the following year) for a calendar year corporation. Corporations can compute their estimated tax payments by using an annualized method similar to the annualized method for individuals.

Usually corporations want to pay estimated taxes for the current year equal to the tax liability shown on the prior year tax return. Then there will not be a penalty even if the tax due for the current year is substantially in excess of the estimates paid. To avoid penalties under the estimated tax rules, corporations must have filed a tax return reflecting a 12-month period in the prior year and must have had a tax liability in the prior year.

Large corporations, corporations with $1 million of taxable income in one of the three preceding tax years, may not pay estimated taxes based upon the amount of tax paid in the prior year. That means that such large corporations must review their taxable income during the year and make estimated tax payments based upon projected income.

A new corporation will have to pay estimated tax for federal purposes when it is anticipated that its estimated tax for the year will be $40 or more. If a corporation anticipates operating at a loss for the first year, no federal estimates will be due.

It is different in some states, such as California. California has a minimum tax that must be paid even if the corporation has a loss for the first year or any year.

New corporations organized and qualified to do business in California must pay a minimum fee at the time of incorporation or qualification. This fee is for the privilege of doing business in California in its first year.

In addition to the incorporation fee paid to the Secretary of State, a new corporation must make an estimated tax payment in the amount of the minimum tax. The minimum tax is:

Corporate Estimated Taxes

Important

Year Beginning In	Amount
1989	$600
1990 and subsequent years	$800

Table 9.1

Tax Tip

Care should be taken in determining when an entity is incorporated. If an entity is incorporated on June 5 and plans to have a June fiscal year end, it incurs an unnecessary minimum tax if it does not conduct business in June. If the entity were not incorporated until July, the extra minimum tax payment may be avoided.

The difference between the total tax due and the estimated tax payments made for a tax year must be paid when the corporate tax return is filed or extended on the 15th day of the 3rd month following the end of the tax year (March 15 for calendar year corporations). A corporate tax return is filed or extended one month earlier than an individual income tax return.

Corporate Income Tax Returns — Forms 1120 and 1120S

Important

A corporation must file a tax return even though the corporation has no income or tax due.

Corporate returns must be filed or extended by the 15th day of the 3rd month following the tax year end of the corporation (March 15 for a calendar year corporation). If the tax for the year is paid, a return can be "extended" (not filed) for an additional six months. California allows an additional seven months rather than six months.

Points to Remember

1   A corporation having taxable income for a year will have to pay estimated taxes throughout the year.

2   Four estimated tax payments are required.

3   If the corporation does not earn income during the first part of the year, it may compute estimated tax payments in the latter part of the year based upon an annualized income.

4   A corporation can also avoid penalties by paying current year estimates equal to the tax shown on the return for the prior year.

5   Any balance of the tax due for the current year must be paid when the tax return is due.

6   New corporations will have to estimate their income for the year and make the required estimated taxes based upon the income for their particular estimate period.

7   Entities incorporated in California must pay a fee when they incorporate and pay a minimum estimated tax for the first tax year, even though the corporation may have a loss for the year.

8   Corporations are required to file annual tax returns even if they have no income or taxes due.

CHAPTER

TEN

_____

Individual
Tax Rules

Individual Tax Rules

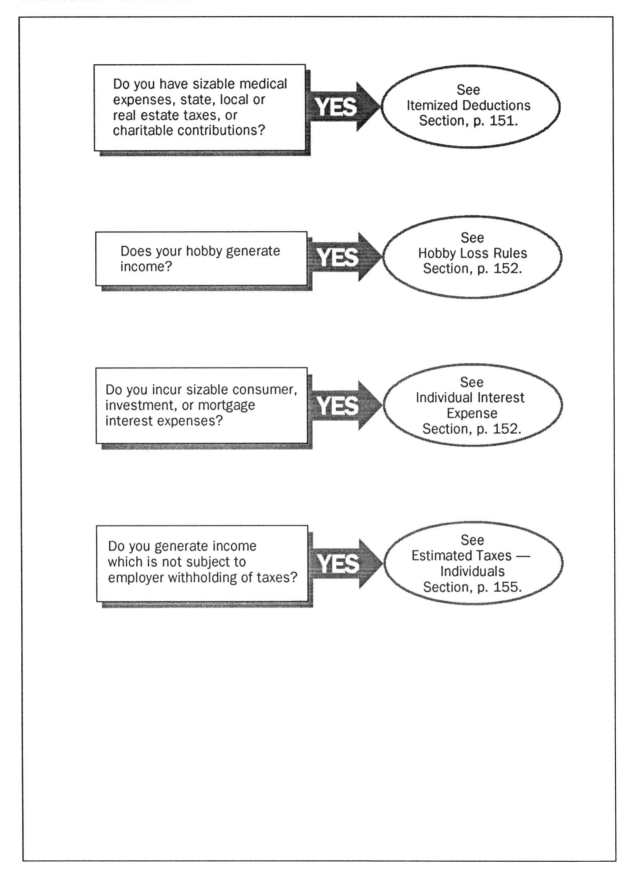

This section covers deductions and items that are unique to individual taxation. It is not a complete analysis of all the rules that apply to individuals. (That would take volumes rather than a mere chapter!) We touch on those rules that may be of most interest to small business owners.

The tax laws allow deductions for certain expenditures that are not related to a trade, business, or investment. These expenses are generally deducted as itemized deductions by individuals. Medical expenses, including prescriptions and doctors fees, are deductible but only to the extent that your aggregate medical expenditures in any one year exceed 7.5% of your adjusted gross income.

Adjusted gross income is essentially the total amount of income received by an individual, less business losses and other deductions. If an individual's adjusted gross income is $100,000, only medical expenses in excess of $7,500 will be deductible.

State and local income taxes are deductible for federal purposes but not for state purposes. Real estate taxes are deductible. Real estate taxes paid on business property are deductible as a business expense rather than an itemized deduction. The deduction for sales tax was eliminated with the 1986 Tax Reform Act.

Charitable contributions are deductible. However, the deduction is limited in certain situations. Limitations are based upon the type of organization to which the contribution is made and the type of property donated. Contributions to public charities can be deducted to the extent of 50% of the taxpayer's adjusted gross income. The fair market value of the gift is the amount deductible. Amounts that are not deductible because of the limitation may be carried forward for five years.

The charitable contribution rules are very complex and advice of a CPA or attorney needs to be secured prior to making a contribution of substantial size.

A casualty loss from a nonbusiness asset is deductible to the extent the loss exceeds $100. In addition to the $100 floor, to be deductible casualty losses must exceed 10% of an individual's adjusted gross income. A casualty loss is a loss that arises from an event that is sudden and unexpected or from an unusual cause. Losses attributable to hurricanes, floods, vandalism, or earthquakes are casualty losses.

1 Individuals can deduct certain expenditures that are not trade, business, or investment expenses. Such expenses are deducted as itemized deductions.

2 Itemized deductions include among others: medical expenses, state and local income taxes, real estate taxes, charitable contributions, and casualty losses.

3 There are various limitations with respect to the various itemized deductions.

Itemized Deductions

Caution

Points to Remember

Hobby Loss Rules

Losses from hobby activities, i.e., activities for which there is no profit motive, are generally deductible only to the extent of the income generated by the activity. If an activity has profit in three out of five consecutive years, the tax laws presume the activity is not a hobby. However, the IRS may rebut the presumption and argue that an activity is a hobby. If so, the expenses can be deducted only to the extent of the income generated by the activity. They cannot create a tax loss.

Points to Remember

1   Losses from hobbies are deductible only to the extent of the income generated by the hobby.

Individual Interest Expense

The current interest expense rules mandate that you first determine the type of interest expense. If the interest expense is investment interest, it can only be deducted to the extent of investment income. Investment interest expense is interest on debt incurred to purchase or continue to own an investment asset such as stocks, bonds, or other investments.

Interest expense attributable to the acquisition or the continued ownership of a passive activity is deemed to be part of the income or loss from the passive activity. If the activity produces a profit, the interest expense decreases the profit. If the passive activity generates a loss, the interest increases the loss. It may or may not be deductible subject to the passive activity loss rules.

Interest on debt secured by your personal residence is deductible if the debt on which the interest is paid is "acquisition indebtedness" or "home equity" debt. Acquisition indebtedness is debt incurred to acquire, construct, or substantially improve your principal or second residence. Interest may only be deducted on up to $1 million of acquisition indebtedness.

Important

Once the acquisition indebtedness is reduced because of payments applied to principal, it cannot be increased by "refinancing."

A home equity loan is a loan secured by your principal or second residence as long as the home equity and acquisition indebtedness do not exceed the fair market value of the property.

Caution

Home equity loans may not exceed $100,000.

The proceeds from a home equity loan can be used for any purpose. By using a home equity loan, the interest is deductible even if the proceeds are used for consumer purchases.

These rules were enacted as part of the Revenue Act of 1987 and apply to 1988 and subsequent years. A grandfather provision was enacted which treats any debt that was incurred prior to October 14, 1987, and secured by a personal residence, as acquisition indebtedness. The interest that is paid on such debt is deductible, even if the loan proceeds were used for other than the purchase or improvement of a personal residence. Such debt can be refinanced after October 13, 1987 and continue to be grandfathered-acquisition indebtedness. However, the refinancing must not exceed the principal amount of the refinanced debt immediately before the refinancing.

Trade or business interest is any interest incurred to acquire or continue to own a trade or business.

Trade or business interest is not subject to limitations. For example, interest on a line of credit used for working capital in a sole proprietorship is deductible and not subject to any limitations.

Important

Consumer interest is any interest other than the aforementioned types of interest. Consumer interest is no longer deductible. However, the loss of the deduction for such interest expense is phased out so that the following percentage of consumer interest is deductible:

Percent	Year
20	1989
10	1990
0	1991 and after

Table 10.1

1 Interest expense is classified as one of the following: investment, passive activity, personal residence, trade or business, or consumer interest.

Points to Remember

2 There are various rules, limits, and phase-outs for each particular kind of interest.

3 Investment interest can only be deducted to the extent of investment income.

4 Passive activity interest is treated as part of the profit or loss from the passive activity and subject to the passive activity rules.

5 Personal residence interest is deductible as an itemized deduction.

6 Trade or business interest is deductible, and consumer interest is not deductible.

7 The deduction for consumer interest is phased out through 1990.

Employers must "withhold" on compensation payments made to employees. The employer must withhold income taxes based on certain exemptions, etc., as reflected on an employee's Form W-4. The purpose of the income tax withholding is to have employees satisfy their income tax requirements on a pay-as-you-go basis. As indicated below, taxes are satisfied on nonemployee income through estimated tax payments. In addition to withholding income tax, employers must withhold Social Security (FICA) taxes from an employee's compensation, and the employer must make an equal contribution of Social Security taxes on behalf of the employee. Similarly, an employer must pay federal unemployment tax (FUTA). There is no contribution by the employee of unemployment taxes.

The amount to be withheld from an employee's compensation and the like amount to be contributed to Social Security on behalf of an employee is 7.65% (both employer and employee) of up to $51,300 of an employee's compensation ($3,924.45 each). Compensation in excess of such an amount is not subject to Social Security tax. The contribution by an employer to unemployment tax may be as high as 6.2% of an employee's salary, up to $7,000. Generally, tax rates and amounts increase each year.

Common Paymaster Rules

Salary paid by a corporate employer to an employee/shareholder of the corporation is subject to income tax and Social Security tax withholding as indicated above. For various business and economic reasons, business owners sometimes conduct their business through more than one corporation that they or their business associates own. For example, a business owner may conduct business in the State of Nevada through his/her wholly owned corporation and conduct a similar business in the State of California through another corporation which is also 100% owned. This may be done for liability reasons or as required by state law, etc. Because each corporation is an employer, each corporation will have to pay the employer's share of Social Security tax on wages paid to the employee/shareholder. This may result in the employer's share of Social Security tax ($3,924.45) being paid twice — once by each corporate employer. The double payment of the employer's share of Social Security taxes may be reduced by having a "common paymaster" make the compensation payments to the employee/shareholder for each corporate employer. In such a case there is only one employer payment of Social Security tax. Detailed rules exist for taking advantage of the common paymaster rules. The tax statute authorizing the common paymaster rules only applies to corporate employers which are directly or indirectly owned by the same individuals. It may be possible, however, to apply the common paymaster rules concept in some situations where the common ownership requirement is not met and in other business arrangements, such as partnerships, trusts and nonbusiness related payments, such as those to domestic servants by related individuals.

Example

Wanda Worried is in the chemical manufacturing business. She manufactures a highly caustic chemical used in Silicon Valley through her wholly owned corporation, Red Flag. She manufactures a household solvent in Reno, Nevada, through her wholly owned corporation, Wonderful Stuff. Both corporations pay Wanda $100,000 in deductible salary each year. Pursuant to a common paymaster agreement, one corporation pays the entire $200,000 compensation and is reimbursed by the other corporation. The employer's share of Social Security tax is $3,924.45. Had the compensation not been paid by the common paymaster, each corporate employer would have to pay $3,924.45 as the employer's Social Security contribution for the benefit of the employee. Thus, through the common paymaster rules, $3,924.45 is saved.

Example

Tax obligations are met on a pay-as-you-go basis. This is accomplished either through withholding from salary or by paying estimated taxes on business and other income that is not subject to withholding. Estimated tax payments must be made by individuals on the following dates:

Estimated Taxes — Individuals

	Due Date	**Table 10.2**
First Estimate	April 15	
Second Estimate	June 15	
Third Estimate	September 15	
Fourth Estimate	January 15 of the following year	

Penalties will be assessed if the proper amount of estimates and withholding are not paid during the tax year.

Caution

Penalties will not be assessed if 90% of the tax for the tax year is paid in four equal installments (or through withholding) on the dates set forth above. Penalties will not be assessed if the tax paid during the year is equal to the tax shown on the return for the preceding year, provided: (1) a return was filed showing a tax liability for the preceding year and (2) the year consisted of a 12-month period.

A third method to avoid estimated tax penalties is to pay estimates when due based on the annualized income for the period reflected in the installment. Annualization is a process of (1) determining the income for the period ending preceding the estimate due date and (2) determining what that income would be for a full taxable year, if earned at the same rate. A tax is then computed on such hypothetical income. A percentage (as set forth below) of that tax must then be paid on the estimate due date.

Table 10.3   **Percentage**

First Estimate	22.%
Second Estimate	45.
Third Estimate	67.5
Fourth Estimate	90.

Example

Iron Mike is a professional wrestler. He has various contracts with promoters to wrestle. He is not an employee. There is no obligation on the part of the promoters to withhold taxes from compensation payments made to Iron Mike. Iron Mike also has ample passive income (interest and dividends). He anticipates his income will increase in 1990.

Iron Mike will make four estimated tax payments for 1990 equal to one-fourth of the total tax liability for 1989. If additional tax is due for the tax year, it must be paid on April 15, 1991 when the tax return for 1990 is due or is extended.

If Iron Mike thought his income would decrease, he could make four equal estimates. As long as the estimates equalled 90% of his tax liability for 1990, there would not be any penalties.

Alternatively, he could annualize his income and make estimated tax payments based on the annualization.

California rules are essentially the same as the federal rules except that to avoid penalties, an individual is only required to pay 80% of the current year's tax during the year rather than the 90% required by federal law.

Points to Remember

1   You must pay your taxes for the tax year on a pay-as-you-go basis. This is done through withholding payments on an employee's salary and through estimated payments on other income.

2   The four estimated payments have to be made throughout the tax year on specified dates.

3   A taxpayer can pay the tax shown on the prior year's return throughout the current year and avoid any tax penalties if additional tax is due on April 15, when the income tax return must be filed or extended.

Filing Requirements — Individual Income Tax Returns (Form 1040)

Single individuals must file if their income is more than $4,950. Married individuals filing a joint return must file if their income is more than $8,900. If an individual has net earnings from self-employment of $400 or more, a tax return must be filed even if the minimum amount of income, explained above, is not received by the person. The 1040 is due on the 15th day of the 4th month following the tax year end (April 15 for calendar year taxpayers).

Points to Remember

1 Individual tax returns must be filed or extended by April 15 for calendar year taxpayers.

2 A return is due for individuals who have income in excess of $4,950.

3 A return is due if married individuals filing a joint return have income in excess of $8,900.

4 A return must be filed if an individual has net earnings from self-employment of $400 or more.

Tax Planning

CPAs, attorneys, and other professionals specialize in helping individuals and small businesses in tax planning. Tax planning consists of reviewing potential transactions to determine how it should be structured for the best tax results. For example, should an asset be sold this year or next year? Good tax planning may tell you that it is best to sell the property in a subsequent year because there is no tax advantage if the sale is made this year.

A major part of the tax planning process is selecting the proper vehicle or form in which a business should be operated. You may prefer to operate in corporate form to limit your potential liability. At the same time you may want to be treated as an individual for tax purposes. You would elect to do business as an S Corporation.

Planning for estate and gift taxes is also a major area that small business owners should consider. The estate tax is assessed at a 55% rate on taxable estates in excess of $3 million. Unless a small business owner properly plans the transfer of his/her business and other assets, the government may get more than half of the value of the estate! Wouldn't you rather see your children, other family members, friends, or a charity get the assets?

Small business owners probably cannot afford to consult a CPA or attorney or other tax professional on a constant basis, especially when the business is just beginning. However, after reading this book the small business owner should be able to zero in on questions that need to be asked of tax professionals. Once the small business becomes successful, it would be advisable to establish a working relationship with a tax professional and to review new transactions and the continued operation of the business so as to get the best tax results or at least avoid the worst tax results.

CHAPTER

ELEVEN

Sales and Use Tax

Sales and Use Tax

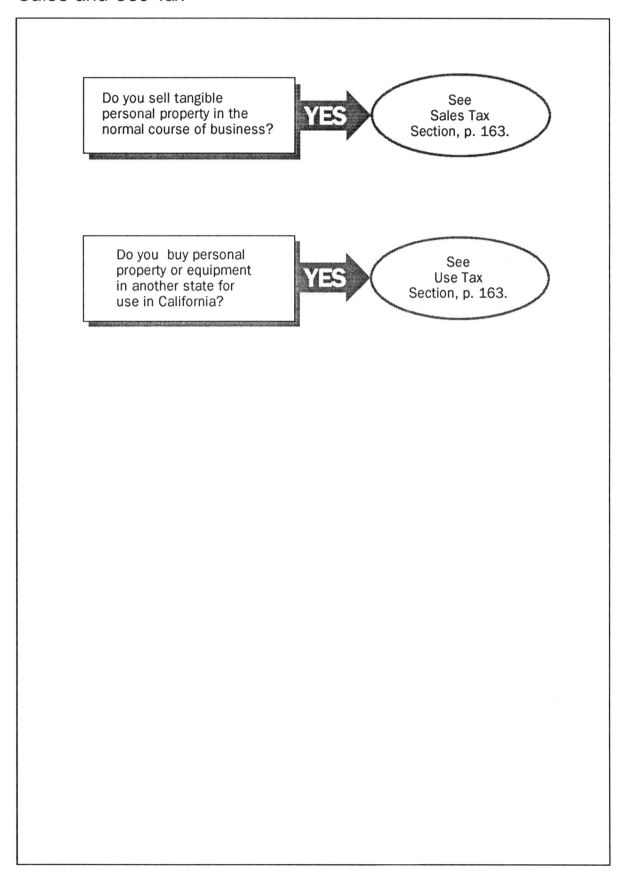

Income taxes are not your only potential tax liability. Individuals and businesses may have to pay a sales tax or a use tax as well. These taxes are levied by California (and most other states) and are a major source of revenue for states. The sales tax is imposed on a retailer for the privilege of selling tangible personal property in a retail business. It is usually passed on to the buyer. The tax is a percentage of the retailer's gross receipts from sales in California.

A retail sale is the sale to anyone who is not going to resell the property in the regular course of the buyer's business. If ties are sold to an individual or business which plans to resell them in its business, the sales tax is not assessed. It is collected when the ties are sold to the final consumer.

Tangible personal property is broadly defined by the state tax authorities. Some sales that one might think are not tangible personal property are deemed tangible personal property for sales or use tax purposes. The sales are then subject to the sales or use tax. The sales tax does not apply to a sale for use outside of California if delivery and transfer of title to the property takes place outside of California.

The use tax is imposed in California on tangible personal property purchased from any retailer outside of California for storage, use or other consumption in California. Like the sales tax, it is assessed as a percentage of the sales price of the property. It generally applies when property is purchased outside of California and brought into California for use.

Example

If an individual goes to Nevada and purchases a car for use primarily in California, it is subject to the California use tax. It is not subject to the California sales tax if it is not purchased within California.

Points to Remember

1   A business may have to pay sales and use taxes.

2   A sales tax must be paid by a business when it sells tangible property to a buyer who is not going to re-sell the product in the ordinary course of business.

3   A business has to pay a use tax if it buys property from outside California for use in California.

Gift, Estate, and Real Property Taxes

Gift, Estate, and Real Property Taxes

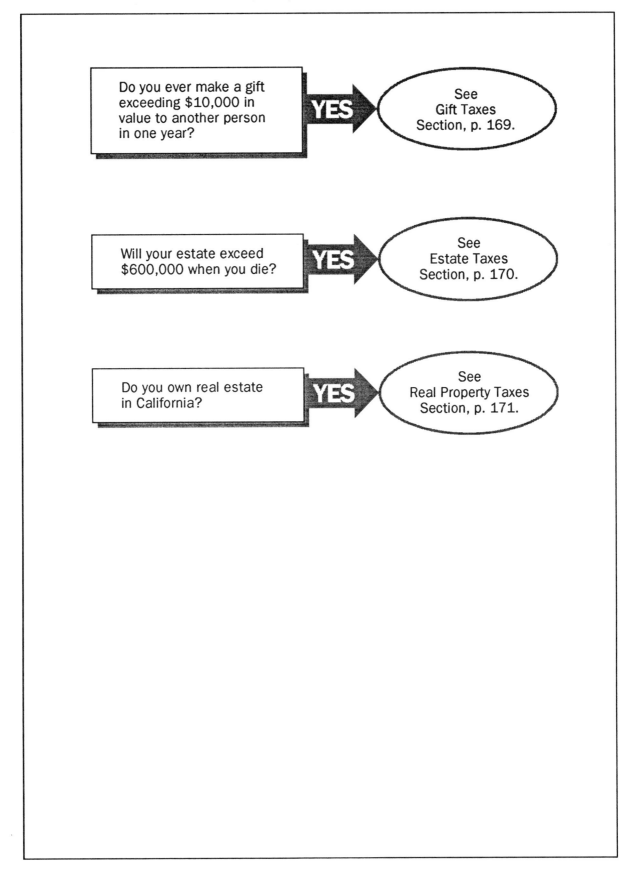

If you transfer assets by gift during your life or at death either as cash or in the form of property, you may have to pay a gift or estate tax. While there may not be a state gift tax payable by a person making a gift, there is a federal gift tax.

A gift tax is due when an amount in excess of $10,000 is gifted by one individual in a calendar year to another person.

An individual can give away $10,000 to any number of people each year free of gift tax. There are exceptions to this rule if the gift is of a future interest; that is, a gift that does not take effect until a subsequent period.

Important

In your lifetime you can give away $600,000 of value, free of the federal gift tax. This is in addition to the $10,000 that can be given annually without incurring a gift tax. This $600,000 amount is reached by allowing a credit against the gift tax for gifts up to $600,000.

A gift tax return must be filed by the individual making the gift when the gifts in any one year exceed the $10,000 per donee limit.

Corporations generally cannot make gifts to individuals. If a gift is made by a corporation, it is treated as a distribution to the shareholder making the gift (and probably subject to income tax). It is also treated as a gift by the shareholder to the individual who receives the gift.

Caution

Gifts to public charities and gifts to one's spouse are treated as taxable gifts but a deduction of the amount given to the charity or spouse is allowed. This essentially means that there is no tax for such gifts but a gift tax return does have to be filed.

A husband and wife can elect to have gifts made by one spouse as made one-half by each spouse.

One spouse can give $20,000 of his/her own property and treat the gift as made one-half by each spouse. Since each spouse is treated as having given $10,000, no tax is due. A gift tax return has to be filed to elect to split the gift.

Example

If property is treated as community property for local law purposes, you can only give away your individual interest in the community property. The split gift election (technique set forth in the example above) does not apply if the property is community property.

If a married couple, Harry and Peabody, give their graduating daughter a new car, the gift will be treated as made one-half by each spouse if the funds used to purchase the car are community property funds.

Example

Community property assets include wages earned during a marriage and any assets purchased with such wages. Gifts and inheritances are separate property of the person receiving them. Assets owned prior to marriage generally remain separate assets. Separate assets can become community assets if commingled.

Estate Taxes

If you die leaving substantial assets in your taxable estate, an estate tax may be due to the Federal Government and the State of California.[1] The federal and California estate taxes are based upon the value of the assets in the decedent's taxable estate at death.

The federal estate tax is levied on net assets in the estate in excess of $600,000. The $600,000 amount is reduced by gifts that are made during life and not taxed because of the $600,000 credit, as explained above under gift taxes.

The California estate tax is the amount of credit allowed under the federal estate tax rules for taxes paid to a state.

As with gifts, there is a deduction from the estate for gifts made to a charity and to a surviving spouse. If all of a decedent's property is transferred to the surviving spouse, there will not be an estate tax on the assets in the decedent's estate. The assets may be subject to the estate tax when the surviving spouse dies depending on the size of the estate at death.

Tax Tip

If the combined estate of a husband and wife is $1,200,000, the first spouse to die should give his/her property to the other spouse in trust so that such property is not included in the estate of the second spouse to die. This way, $1,200,000 can be given away without gift or estate tax. Otherwise, only $600,000 would escape such taxes.

Example

Wanda and Xavier have a community property estate of $1,200,000. Wanda expires and leaves her $600,000 in trust to Xavier. The terms of the trust are that Xavier will have the income from the trust for life. On his death the trust assets will be distributed to Yale. Xavier can also use the assets or principal of the trust for his support, maintenance, health, or education.

On Xavier's death the $600,000 in the trust will not be included in his estate. Thus, each spouse has transferred $600,000—a total of $1,200,000 free of estate or gift tax.

If Wanda had given her $600,000 to Xavier outright rather than in the trust, only $600,000 would be given away free of estate or death tax when Xavier passed away. This is because Xavier would have had $1,200,000 in his estate but could only transfer $600,000 free of tax.

---

[1] Prior to 1982, an inheritance tax was payable to the State of California instead of an estate tax. The inheritance tax was based upon the relationship of the individual receiving the inheritance to the person who died.

The estate tax rates (as well as the gift tax rates) essentially range from 37% to 55%. The 55% rate applies to taxable estates (and taxable gifts) of $3 million or more. Individuals of substantial wealth need to plan for the estate tax. They need to plan ahead to avoid or defer it, or, at a minimum, to have liquid assets available to pay the estate tax.

1   You may be subject to gift and estate tax liabilities.

2   A gift tax must be paid when gifts of more than $600,000 are made by you in your lifetime.

3   Gifts of $10,000 can be given each year to any number of individuals without counting toward the $600,000.

4   An estate tax is payable when an individual dies with an estate of more than $600,000.

5   Prior gifts are counted as being part of the estate for purposes of the $600,000 amount. You can give away, during your lifetime or upon death, a total of $600,000.

6   The first spouse to die should give his/her assets to the surviving spouse in a trust so they would not be included in the surviving spouse's estate. Otherwise, only $600,000 will escape gift or estate taxation.

Points to Remember

Owners of real property must pay property taxes. Real property taxes must be paid whether the property is a residence, investment property or property used in trade or business.

In California the infamous Proposition 13 substantially limited the ability of the County Assessor to tax real property. The value of the property owned in 1978 was frozen at its March 1978 value, subject to a 2% per year increase for inflation. However, property purchased subsequent to 1978, newly constructed property, or property subject to a "change in ownership" is valued at the time of the purchase, construction, or change in ownership. Again, the tax base may increase 2% per year for inflation. The tax rate is generally limited to 1% of the value of the property. Other states more or less will estimate real property taxes based on the fair market value of real property.

Proposition 13 results in similar property being subject to vastly different taxes and is, thus, being challenged as unconstitutional.

Recently the property tax rules were favorably changed with respect to residences. Under the new rules, persons over 55 can transfer a residence and purchase a new residence as long as the value of the new residence is equal to or lesser than the value of the old residence without increasing the property taxes resulting from the sale and purchase of new property but only if the purchase of the new residence is in the county where the old residence was sold and certain other counties that have elected to allow such roll-over benefit.

Real Property Taxes

New construction requiring revaluation and increased property taxes occurs when there is development of land, additions to an existing building, or other significant changes. The increased value is added to the value prior to the new construction to determine the new value on which the County Assessor can collect taxes.

Important

Keep in mind that a change in ownership can result in substantial increases in property taxes. The effect of Proposition 13 is that 1975 owners of property are not paying much in property taxes if they did not sell or improve the property or have a change of ownership.

A change of ownership occurs when property is sold unless it is sold to your spouse or children. Up to $1 million of other property can be transferred to your children without having a change in ownership and increasing property taxes.

A lease for 35 years or more is deemed a change of ownership. A transfer of real property to a partnership or corporation in which the individuals making the transfer do not own the partnership or corporation in the same percentage as they own the real property transferred is a change of ownership.

There is not a change of ownership for real property owned by a partnership or corporation merely because new partners or shareholders acquire an interest in the partnership or corporation. There is a change of ownership if more than 50% of the ownership of the partnership or corporation changes hands.

Example

Allen and Bill own 100% of D.E.F. corporation. Allen transfers the real property used in the corporation business to the corporation. This is a change in ownership because before the transaction, Allen owned 100% of the real property. After the transfer, he only owned indirectly one-half of the real property.

Important

When there is a sale or other change of ownership, the property will be revalued for tax purposes the month following the change of ownership.

Points to Remember

1   If you own real property, you must pay real property taxes.

2   Since Proposition 13, real property taxes have been somewhat limited.

3   The tax rate is limited to 1% of the value of the property.

4   The value of property owned in 1978 was deemed to be its value for subsequent years, subject to a 2% inflation increase.

5   When there is new construction or a change in ownership, real property taxes are assessed on the value of the property rather than cost plus 2%.

6   A change in ownership takes place when property is sold or transferred to a corporation or partnership in which the

transferors of the real property do not own the same percent of the partnership or corporation as they do in the real property.

7   A change in ownership also takes place if more than 50% of the ownership of a partnership or corporation changes hands.

8   A transfer to your spouse or children is generally not a change of ownership resulting in increased property taxes.

The primary focus of this book has been state and federal income taxation. We briefly touched on sales taxes, real property taxes, and estate taxes. The most important part of this book may be the analysis of the form in which you should conduct your business — sole proprietor, partnership, or corporation and the discussion of basic business issues, do's and don't's. The rest of the book discusses basic income tax issues — for instance, when you can deduct expenses and how you can compute depreciation.

Summary

This book only provides a fundamental analysis, and so there may be obscure points not covered. Also, there are several exceptions to almost every general rule of tax law. Therefore, after making your decision, based upon reading this book, about the best form for your business, you should talk with a CPA or attorney who specializes in taxes. You should also discuss a plan for organizing your books and records. You may be able to take care of this yourself, or you may need a bookkeeper or CPA. If you do not know a CPA or attorney, the state or local CPA Society or Bar Association can provide names of competent tax practitioners. You may also ask your business associates for a recommendation and, finally, consult the yellow pages of the telephone book.

In addition to hiring a CPA or attorney, you might need the services of other professional advisors such as qualified plan administrators, actuaries, etc. You should be able to obtain the names of competent individuals in these areas from the CPA or attorney you select. Your banker may also be able to give you the names of competent advisors. Once your business is growing and successful, you clearly need to take advantage of professional advisors to help you plan to meet your business and financial goals, including paying no more than the required amount of tax.

In addition to taxes, there are other substantial business questions you need to consider when getting started. These were discussed in Chapter 1. You need to lay the groundwork for establishing your business. To do this properly, you will want to research your market, develop a business plan and project your business income and expenses.

You need to consider such financial matters as securing funds to conduct a business. You may decide to buy an existing business or to be a franchisee rather than starting your own business from scratch . Also, you will need to consider buying telephone systems, negotiating leases, hiring employees, advertising, and so on. Your CPA or attorney may be able to help you with these issues — such advisors generally have a wealth of experience from helping other small business clients with these matters.

Various government agencies and trade associations are available to help you. The United States Small Business Administration has a wealth of information and help available for you. They have numerous booklets discussing business issues as well as counselors who can help you with getting started and maintaining your business. You can contact SBA offices at the addresses and telephone numbers in your local telephone book.

The U.S. Department of Commerce may also be helpful as they have many booklets discussing doing business in and competing in foreign markets. You can meet with counselors at the Department of Commerce and they can advise you on various aspects of your business. Local groups such as a city's Office of Business and Economic Development, local small business advisory commissions or state and local chambers of commerce can also be very helpful.

Don't forget your local library and bookstore (where you purchased this invaluable collector's item) — they will have books and other materials on various aspects of business, such as sales and management. Also remember to make business connections by networking at seminars, trade shows and groups. For example, the various committees at the local chamber of commerce may be an invaluable source of information as well as giving you the chance to meet up with potential clients, customers or suppliers.

In addition to general business issues and taxes, there are often local requirements with which businesses have to comply. You may have to file a fictitious business name at the County Clerk's office in the county where you will conduct you business. There may also be local zoning rules or licensing regulations that will affect you. Some local governments require the payment of business taxes. You can get information about such local requirements from the County Clerk or tax collector.

As well as these local jurisdiction requirements, there will be state requirements. If you intend to sell goods, you will probably have to get a seller's permit. States may regulate particular activities and thus you may need a license to conduct this kind of activity. You may also have to pay for workers' compensation insurance.

In summary, in getting started don't overlook the wealth of resources provided by federal, state and local agencies which exist primarily to help you in your business. You should take advantage of all these resources in planning your business. With a lot of hard work and a little luck, you will be a very successful business person. Good luck or, as they say in tax heaven, many happy returns!

Amortization
The deduction using a straight-line method for various intangible costs such as organization expenses, etc.

Annual Lease Value
IRS tables that provide the amount of income to be recognized by individual taxpayers when cars are leased for use in a trade or business.

At Risk
The requirement that a person must have risk funds (cash) invested to take a tax loss from an activity.

Basis
The dollar value of property on which gain or loss on sale and depreciation are computed. Basis is generally cost reduced by depreciation. Generally, the basis of inherited property is its fair market value.

Breach of Contract
The failure to perform the tasks agreed to in a contract with another party or parties.

Built-in-Gain Tax
The tax that is imposed upon certain S Corporations when they sell property that the S Corporation owned and which was appreciated at the time of the S Corporation election.

Cafeteria Plans
Various employee benefits offered to an employee where the employee generally must elect some of the benefits offered but cannot elect to receive all the benefits.

Capital Expenditure
Amounts paid that will benefit future years.

Capital Gain
The excess of proceeds received from the sale or exchange of a non-inventory asset over the cost or other tax basis of the asset.

Closely Held
A corporation that has a few shareholders.

Conformity
The concept of the state tax laws adopting or following the federal tax laws. In the past few years the states rules have adopted or conformed, in part, to the federal tax laws.

Consent
The signing of Form 2553 by the shareholders of the S Corporation, agreeing that the entity can elect to be treated as an S Corporation and that the shareholders rather than the corporation will be taxed on the corporate income.

Glossary

Corporation
A legal entity operating under authority given by a state or other government.

Deferred Compensation
Payment for services rendered when such payment is received substantially after the services are rendered. Taxation of the compensation payments is or may be deferred until payment is actually made.

Depreciation
The tax deduction allowed for property used in a trade or business to reflect the decrease in value of the property.

Estate
The assets directly or indirectly owned by a person at his/her death.

Exclusion from Gross Income
Statutorily provided exceptions to the general rule that income must be recognized when received.

Fair Market Value
The price at which a willing seller and a willing buyer will trade, each being well informed.

Franchise Tax
The tax imposed by states upon income of a corporation, theoretically for the franchise or right of the corporation to conduct business in that state.

General Utilities
The doctrine that prior to the 1986 Tax Reform Act allowed corporations to sell their assets free of corporate level tax and distribute the sales proceeds in liquidation of the corporation.

Gift Tax
The tax owed to the federal government as a result of giving property away.

Gross Income
The amount of revenue before deducting expenses, attributable to earning the revenue.

Gross Profit
The sales price of inventory less the cost of inventory.

Illegal Payment
A payment, such as a bribe, which is unlawful or contrary to law as opposed to payments pertaining to an illegal business.

Imputed Income
Income deemed to be realized and recognized for tax purposes.

Life Insurance Proceeds
The cash received by the beneficiary of a life insurance policy on the death of the person who is insured by the policy.

Liquidate
The process of selling or distributing the assets of the business, settling the debts and distributing the remaining assets or equity to the owners.

Limited Partnership
A Limited Partnership consisting of one or more general partners, which conduct the business of the partnership and who are responsible for the liabilities of the partnership, and limited partners who contribute cash to the partnership and generally do not participate in the management of the partnership or the liabilities of the partnership.

Luxury Automobile
A passenger automobile for which the depreciation deduction allowed by the tax laws is less than the depreciation computed on the cost basis of the car. A car purchased after 1986 is a luxury car if the purchase price exceeds $12,763.

Marginal Tax Rate
The tax rate that applies to the next dollar of earned income. For example, the overall tax rate may be 28% but the next dollar of income may be taxed at the 33% rate.

Net Operating Loss (NOL)
The excess of expenses over income resulting from the conduct of a trade or business.

Nonresident
An individual who has not lived in a state (or county) a sufficient period of time to be deemed a resident. Nonresidents are generally only taxed on income from sources within a state or country rather than on worldwide income.

PAL/PIG
A PAL is a passive activity loss, the deduction of which is generally limited. A PIG is a passive income generator — passive activity income that can be used to absorb passive activity losses.

Partnership
An entity in which the parties carry on their trade or business for the joint benefit and profit of all partners.

Penalty Taxes
Various taxes imposed to penalize taxpayers for certain action or failure to take action. For example, there is an accumulated earnings tax on corporations that fail to distribute their income to the owners.

Professional Corporation
A corporation that conducts a business generally considered to be professional, such as law, medicine, accounting, architecture, engineering, etc.

Realization
A transaction resulting in gain being received although it may not be reorganized or taxable.

Real Property Change in Ownership
The transfer of real property as defined in the state property tax laws that results in the reassessment of the property for real property tax purposes.

Recognized
A transaction giving rise to taxable income or loss rather than unrecognized or deferred, etc.

Repair
The cost of restoring a capital asset after damage or prolonged use.

Reserve
The reduction of income or retained earnings to reflect expenses that may be incurred in the future. For example, a reserve for bad debts is a decrease in income attributable to accounts receivable that may not be collectable.

Resident
For tax purposes, a person who lives in a state (or country) for a sufficient period of time to be termed a resident. Residents are generally taxed on their worldwide income.

Restricted Stock
Stock owned by an individual which generally cannot be sold or otherwise disposed of until certain conditions such as years of employment are met.

Retail
The selling of goods to the ultimate consumer as opposed to wholesale where bulk goods are sold to buyers who resell.

S Corporation
An incorporated entity which has elected to be treated for tax purposes as an S Corporation. Generally, an S Corporation does not pay tax — rather its shareholders pay tax.

Securities
A general term that includes all instruments representing evidence of ownership or debt issued by a company or a corporation. The term securities generally means stocks and bonds.

S Election
The filing of Form 2553 on a timely basis with the federal tax authorities to elect to be treated as an S Corporation for tax purposes.

Sole Proprietor
A business enterprise that belongs entirely to one individual.

Special Allocation of Partnership Income
The agreement amongst the partners in a partnership to allocate income, losses, etc., to the various partners other than pro rata based upon ownership.

Stock Option
The right pursuant to agreement with a corporation to purchase the corporation's stock.

Tangible Personal Property
Property that can be felt and touched and is not real property as opposed to intangible property, such as stocks and bonds which only represent property.

Tort
An injury or wrong done to a person.

Appendices

FINANCIAL MANAGEMENT AND ANALYSIS

FM 1 ABC's OF BORROWING *
Some small business people cannot understand why a lending institution refused to lend them money. Others have no trouble getting funds but are surprised to find strings attached to their loans. Learn the fundamentals of borrowing. $1.00.

**FM 2 PROFIT COSTING
AND PRICING FOR MANUFACTURERS**
Uncover the latest techniques for pricing your products profitably. $1.00.

FM 3 BASIC BUDGETS FOR PROFIT PLANNING *
This publication takes the worry out of putting together a comprehensive budgeting system to monitor your profits and assess your financial operations. $0.50.

FM 4 UNDERSTANDING CASH FLOW
In order to survive, a business must have enough cash to meet its obligations. Learn how to plan for the movement of cash through the business and thus plan for future requirements. $1.00.

**FM 5 A VENTURE CAPITAL PRIMER
FOR SMALL BUSINESS ***
This best-seller highlights the venture capital resources available and how to develop a proposal for obtaining these funds. $0.50.

**FM 6 ACCOUNTING SERVICES
FOR SMALL SERVICE FIRMS**
Sample profit/loss statements are used to illustrate how accounting services can help expose and correct trouble spots in a business's financial records. $0.50.

FM 7 ANALYZE YOUR RECORDS TO REDUCE COSTS
Cost reduction is NOT simply slashing any and all expenses. Understand the nature of expenses and how they inter-relate with sales inventories and profits. Achieve greater profits through more efficient use of the dollar. $0.50.

FM 8 BUDGETING IN A SMALL BUSINESS FIRM
Learn how to set up and keep sound financial records. Study how to effectively use journals, ledgers and charts to increase profits. $0.50.

FM 9 SOUND CASH MANAGEMENT AND BORROWING
Avoid a "cash crisis" through proper use of cash budgets, cash flow projections and planned borrowing concepts. $0.50.

FM 10 RECORDKEEPING IN A SMALL BUSINESS *
Need some basic advice on setting up a useful record keeping system? This publication describes how. $1.00.

**FM 11 BREAKEVEN ANALYSIS:
A DECISION MAKING TOOL.**
Learn how "breakeven analysis" enables the manager/owner to
make better decisions concerning sales, profits and costs. $1.00.

FM 12 A PRICING CHECKLIST FOR SMALL RETAILERS
The owner/manager of a small retail business can use this checklist
to apply proven pricing strategies that can lead to profits. $0.50.

**FM 13 PRICING YOUR PRODUCTS
AND SERVICES PROFITABLY**
Discusses how to price your products profitably, how to use the
various techniques of pricing and when to use these techniques to
your advantage. $1.00.

GENERAL MANAGEMENT AND PLANNING

MP 1 EFFECTIVE BUSINESS COMMUNICATIONS
Explains the importance of business communications and how they
play a valuable role in business success. $0.50.

MP 2 LOCATING OR RELOCATING YOUR BUSINESS
Learn how a company's market, available labor force, availability
of transportation and raw materials are affected by a business's
location. $1.00.

**MP 3 PROBLEMS IN MANAGING
A FAMILY-OWNED BUSINESS**
Specific problems exist when attempting to make a family-owned
business successful. This publication offers suggestions on how to
overcome these difficulties. $0.50.

MP 4 BUSINESS PLAN FOR SMALL MANUFACTURERS
Designed to help an owner/manager of a small manufacturing firm.
This publication covers all the basic information necessary to
develop an effective business plan. $1.00.

**MP 5 BUSINESS PLAN
FOR SMALL CONSTRUCTION FIRMS**
This publication is designed to help an owner/manager of a small
construction company pull together the resources to develop a business plan. $1.00.

**MP 6 PLANNING AND GOAL SETTING
FOR SMALL BUSINESS ***
Learn how to plan for success. $0.50.

MP 7 FIXING PRODUCTION MISTAKES
Structured as a checklist, this publication emphasizes the steps that
should be taken by a manufacturer when a production mistake has
been found. $0.50.

MP 8 SHOULD YOU LEASE OR BUY EQUIPMENT?
Describes various aspects of the lease/buy decision. It lists advantages and disadvantages of leasing and provides a format for comparing the costs of the two. $0.50.

MP 9 BUSINESS PLAN FOR RETAILERS
Learn how to develop a business plan for a retail business. $1.00.

MP 10 CHOOSING A RETAIL LOCATION
Learn about current retail site selection techniques such as demographic and traffic analysis. This publication addresses the hard questions the retailer must answer before making the choice of a store location. $1.00.

MP 11 BUSINESS PLAN FOR SMALL SERVICE FIRMS
Outlines the key points to be included in the business plan of a small service firm. $0.50.

MP 12 GOING INTO BUSINESS *
This best-seller highlights important considerations you should address in reaching a decision to start your own business. It also includes a checklist for going into business. $0.50.

MP 13 FEASIBILITY CHECKLIST
FOR STARTING YOUR OWN BUSINESS
Helps you determine if your idea represents a real business opportunity. Assists you in screening out ideas that are likely to fail before you invest extensive time, money and effort in them. $1.00

MP 14 HOW TO GET STARTED
WITH A SMALL BUSINESS COMPUTER
Helps you forecast your computer needs, evaluate the alternative choices and select the right computer system for your business. $1.00.

MP 15 THE BUSINESS PLAN
FOR HOMEBASED BUSINESS *
Provides a comprehensive approach to developing a business plan for a homebased business. If you are convinced that a profitable home business is attainable, this publication will provide a step-by-step guide to develop a plan for your business. $1.00.

MP 16 HOW TO BUY OR SELL A BUSINESS
Learn several techniques used in determining the best price at which to buy or sell a small business. $1.00.

MP 17 PURCHASING FOR OWNERS OF SMALL PLANTS
Presents an outline of an effective purchasing program. Also includes a bibliography for further research into industrial purchasing. $0.50.

MP 18 BUYING FOR RETAIL STORES
Discusses the latest trends in retail buying. Includes a bibliography that references a wide variety of private and public sources of information on most aspects of retail buying. $1.00.

MP 19 SMALL BUSINESS DECISION MAKING
Acquaint yourself with the wealth of information available on management approaches to identify, analyze and solve business problems. $1.00.

MP 20 BUSINESS CONTINUATION PLANNING
Provides an overview of business owner's life insurance needs that are not typically considered until after the death of one of the business's principal owners. $1.00.

MP 21 DEVELOPING A STRATEGIC BUSINESS PLAN *
Helps you develop a strategic action plan for your small business. $1.00.

MP 22 INVENTORY MANAGEMENT
Discusses the purpose of inventory management, types of inventories, record keeping and forecasting inventory levels. $0.50.

MP 23 TECHNIQUES FOR PROBLEM SOLVING
Instructs the small business person on the key techniques of problem solving and problem identification, as well as designing and implementing a plan to correct these problems. $1.00.

MP 24 TECHNIQUES
FOR PRODUCTIVITY IMPROVEMENT
Learn to increase worker output through motivating quality of work life concepts and tailoring benefits to meet the needs of the employees. 1.00.

MP 25 SELECTING THE LEGAL STRUCTURE
FOR YOUR BUSINESS
Discusses the various legal structures that a small business can use in setting up its operations. It briefly identifies the types of legal structures and lists the advantages and disadvantages of each. $0.50.

MP 26 EVALUATING FRANCHISE OPPORTUNITIES
Although the success rate for franchise owned businesses is significantly better than start-up businesses, success is not guaranteed. Evaluate franchise opportunities and select the business that's right for you. $0.50.

CRIME PREVENTION

CP 1 REDUCING SHOPLIFTING LOSSES
Learn the latest techniques on how to spot, deter, apprehend and prosecute shoplifters. $0.50.

CP 2 CURTAILING CRIME — INSIDE AND OUT
Positive steps CAN be taken to curb crime. They include safe-
guards against employee dishonesty and ways to control shoplift-
ing. In addition, this publication includes measures to outwit bad
check passing and ways to prevent burglary and robbery. $1.00.

CP 3 A SMALL BUSINESS
GUIDE TO COMPUTER SECURITY
The computer is a valuable and essential part of many small businesses, and your computer related assets need protection. This publication helps you understand the nature of computer security risks
and offers timely advice on how to control them. $1.00.

MARKETING

MT 1 CREATIVE SELLING: THE COMPETITIVE EDGE*
Explains how to use creative selling techniques to increase profits.
$0.50

MT 2 MARKETING FOR SMALL BUSINESS:
AN OVERVIEW*
Provides an overview of "Marketing" concepts and contains an
extensive bibliography of sources covering the subject of marketing. $1.00

MT 3 IS THE INDEPENDENT SALES AGENT FOR YOU?
Provides guidelines that help the owner of a small company determine if a sales agent is needed and pointers on how to choose one.
$0.50

MT 4 MARKETING CHECKLIST
FOR SMALL RETAILERS
This checklist is for the owner/manager of a small retail business.
The questions outlined cover customer analysis, buying, pricing
and promotions and other factors in the retail marketing process.
$1.00

MT 5 ADVERTISING GUIDELINES
FOR SMALL RETAIL FIRMS
Guidelines include how to plan an advertising budget, select appropriate media, use cooperative advertising and prepare advertisements. $0.50.

MT 6 ADVERTISING MEDIA DECISIONS *
Discover how to effectively target your product or service to the
proper market. This publication also discusses the different advertising media and how to select and use the best media vehicle for
your business. $1.00.

MT 7 PLAN YOUR ADVERTISING BUDGET

Describes methods for establishing an advertising budget and suggests ways of changing budget amounts to get the effect you want. $0.50.

MT 8 RESEARCH YOUR MARKET *

Learn what market research is and how you can benefit from it. Introduces inexpensive techniques that small business owners can apply to gather facts about their customer base and how to expand it. $1.00.

MT 9 SELLING BY MAIL ORDER

Provides basic information on how to run a successful mail order business. Includes information on product selection, pricing, testing and writing effective advertisements. $1.00.

MT 10 MARKET OVERSEAS
WITH U.S. GOVERNMENT HELP

Entering the overseas marketplace offers exciting opportunities to increase company sales and profits. Learn about the programs available to help small businesses break into the world of exporting. $1.00.

PERSONNEL MANAGEMENT

PM 1 CHECKLIST FOR DEVELOPING A TRAINING PROGRAM

Describes a step-by-step process of setting up an effective employee training program. $0.50.

PM 2 EMPLOYEES: HOW TO FIND AND PAY THEM

A business is only as good as the people in it. Learn how to find and hire the right employees. $1.00.

PM 3 MANAGING EMPLOYEE BENEFITS

Describes employee benefits as one part of the total compensation package and discusses proper management of benefits. $1.00.

NEW PRODUCTS/IDEAS/INVENTIONS

PL 1 CAN YOU MAKE MONEY
WITH YOUR IDEA OR INVENTION?

This publication is a step-by-step guide which shows how you can make money by turning your creative ideas into marketable products. It is a resource for entrepreneurs attempting to establish themselves in the marketplace. $0.50.

PL 2 INTRODUCTION TO PATENTS
Offers some basic facts about patents to help clarify your rights. It discusses the relationships among a business, an inventor and the Patent and Trademark Office to ensure protection of your product and to avoid or win infringement suits. $0.50.

* Denotes a best-seller.

How to Order
1. Include publication number and title, and make your check or money order payable to: U.S. Small Business Administration (NOTE: No cash, credit cards or purchase orders please!)
2. Mail to:
    U.S. Small Business Administration
    P.O. Box 15434
    Fort Worth, Texas 76119

Appendix II
Business Plan
Checklist

The business plan should tell a complete story about your business. It is primarily used by yourself as a roadmap and should be considered a living document to be reviewed and updated every 3-6 months. If you do need a loan, your banker will appreciate the indepth knowledge of your business which you display with this plan. Here is the suggested S.B.A. format.

Product/Service (Write about 2 pages)
Describe in your own words, as clearly as possible:

a. What products or services you will provide.
b. How many days per week you will be open for business.
c. Hours of operation.
d. Approximate number of clients to be serviced per day.
e. How does your product/service differ from other similar products on the market.
f. How will the loan affect the product/service.

Market (Write about 2 pages)
It is very important to know where your clients or customers are coming from and what kind of people they are.

a. Who will you sell to? Retailers? Wholesalers? The public?
b. Who will be the final customers of the product/service you offer?
c. Where are they located?
d. How many are they?
e. Describe them — what is their average income?
f. Are they family people? Single? Retired?
g. What kind of lifestyle do they lead?
h. How much money can you expect them to spend on this type of product/ service?
i. Why will the above customers want to buy your product/service?
j. What is your expected share of this market? — How many of these customers do you expect to reach?
l. Will the loan affect the share of the market you presently have (if you are already in business)? How?

Location of Business (Write about 1/2 to 1 page)
a. Explain where the business will be located.
b. Is this location easily accessible by automobile traffic, foot traffic?
c. Is there parking available for the customers?
d. What kind of businesses are around your location or close by.
e. Any other information to describe the building.
f. Include any maps showing location of business and location of closest competitors.
g. Explain the type of lease.

Competition (Write about 1 page)
It is very important that you know you competitors.

a. Where is your competition located?
b. How far from you?
c. How many competitors are there? — Give names if possible.
d. How profitable is their business.
e. How are they different from your business.
f. Do you expect to take sales away from these competitors? How?

Distribution (Write about 1 page)

It is very important that you know how to reach your customers and what kind of media you will use for advertising.

a. How will you reach the people you sell to?
b. Would you use sales representatives? Mail orders?
c. How would you let people know about your product/service?
d. Would you advertise? Where?
e. Would you use any other methods? Direct mail; personal contact; flyers; etc.
f. If you have any unique marketing ideas, we would like you to write them down under this category.

Sales (Write at least 1 page)

This section has to do with your projected sales.

a. What will be your total monthly and annual sales for the first year of operation, after you receive the loan?
b. What will be your cost of sales (cost of merchandise or materials)?
c. What is the basis for your cost of sales figure?
d. What percentage of your sales is the cost of sales?
e. What will your average total expenses per month be?
f. How much money do you need to draw per month for personal expenses?
9. How will the loan affect your sales (if you are already in business)?
h. How much will you have to sell to break even?
i. What could seriously change these sales projections (changes in the economy, changes in demand, etc.)?

Key Personnel

This has to do with people working at your business.

a. Who will be in charge of the business operation?
b. How many employees will you have? Give name of position or title.
c. Describe duties and qualifications of each employee, including years of experience in assigned position.
d. Include personal resume of any employee who will have any administrative responsibilities, such as manager or assistant manager or any other employee with authority in your business.
e. Include information in c and d about the owner(s).

Organization

a. What type of organization are you? (corporation, partnership, sole proprietorship).
b. If a corporation, who is on the Board of Directors?
c. If a partnership, who are the partners? (Give percentage of ownership.)
d. Where are the headquarters of the business?
e. Do short term and long term personal goals of the owner(s) harmonize with the business requirements and objectives?

States recognizing some form of S Corporation status:

Appendix III

Alabama	Iowa	North Carolina
Alaska	Kansas	North Dakota
Arizona	Kentucky	Ohio
Arkansas	Maine	Oklahoma
California	Maryland	Oregon
Colorado	Massachusetts	Pennsylvania
Delaware	Minnesota	Rhode Island
Florida	Mississippi	South Carolina
Georgia	Missouri	Utah
Hawaii	Montana	Vermont
Idaho	Nebraska	Virginia
Illinois	New Mexico	West Virginia
Indiana	New York	Wisconsin

Appendix IV

State Personal Income Tax Rates
(% maximum marginal rate-joint return):

Alabama	5%	Maine	8.5%	North Dakota	
Arizona	8%	Maryland	5%		14.57%
Arkansas	7%	Massachusetts		Ohio	6.9%
California	9.3		5.375%	Oklahoma	10%
Colorado	5.5%	Michigan	4.6%	Oregon	9%
Delaware	7.7%	Minnesota	8.5%	Pennsylvania	2.1%
D.C.	9.5%	Mississippi	5%	Rhode Island	
Georgia	6%	Missouri	6%		22.96%
Hawaii	10%	Montana	11%	South Carolina	7%
Idaho	8.2%	Nebraska	5.9%	Tennessee	6%
Illinois	3%	New Hampshire		Utah	7.2%
Indiana	3.4%		5%	Vermont	25%
Iowa	9.98%	New Jersey	3.5%	Virginia	5.75%
Kansas	8.75%	New Mexico	8.5%	West Virginia	6.5%
Kentucky	6%	New York	7.875%	Wisconsin	6.93%
Lousiana	6%	North Carolina	7%		

All states except the following generally use Federal Income as the
state tax base: Alabama, Arkansas, Mississippi, New Jersey, and
Pennsylvania. New Hampshire and Tennessee only tax interest and
dividend income.

Massachusetts taxes interest dividends at a 10% rate. Rhode
Island's tax is 22.9% of the federal income tax liability and
Vermont's is 25% of the federal income tax liability. Michigan
taxes business income at 2.35%.

State Corporate Maximum Marginal Income Tax Rates: Appendix V

Alabama	9.4%	Kentucky	7.25%	North Carolina	7%
Alaska	9.4%	Lousiana	8%	North Dakota	
Arizona	10.5%	Maine	8.93%		110.5%
Arkansas	6%	Maryland	7%	Ohio	8.9%
California	9.3	Massachusetts		Oklahoma	5%
Colorado	5.5%		9.5%	Oregon	6.6%
Connecticut	11.5%	Michigan	2.35%	Pennsylvania	8.5%
Delaware	8.7%	Minnesota	9.5%	Rhode Island	9%
D.C.	15%	Mississippi	5%	South Carolina	5%
Florida	5.5%	Missouri	5%	Tennessee	6%
Georgia	6%	Montana	11.75%	Utah	5%
Hawaii	6.4%	Nebraska	6.65%	Vermont	8.25%
Idaho	8%	New Hampshire		Virginia	6%
Illinois	7%		8%	West Virginia	
Indiana	3.4%	New Jersey	9.375%		9.45%
Iowa	12%	New Mexico	7.6%	Wisconsin	7.9%
Kansas	6.75%	New York	9%		

Michigan taxes business income whether corporate, individual, etc. at a 2.35% rate.

Appendix VI

States using Uniform Division of Income for Tax Purposes Act (UDITPA) for purposes of apportioning income:

Alabama	Indiana	North Dakota
Alaska	Kansas	Oregon
Arizona	Kentucky	Pennsylvania
Arkansas	Maine	Rhode Island
California	Massachusetts	South Carolina
Colorado	Michigan	Tennessee
Washington, D.C.	Missouri	Utah
Florida	Montana	Vermont
Hawaii	Nebraska	Virginia
Idaho	New Mexico	Wisconsin
Illinois	North Carolina	

Colorado and Missouri allow taxpayers to use UDITPA or states' different method.

General Business Forms

Application for Employer Identification Number   SS-4

Fictitious Business Name Statement   California

Individual Tax Forms — Federal

U.S. Individual Income Tax Form   1040

Itemized Deductions and Interest and Dividend Income
    Schedules A & B (1040)

Profit or Loss from Business   Schedule C (1040)

Alternative Minimum Tax Individuals   6251

Application for Automatic Extension of Time to File U.S.
    Individual Tax Return   4868

Partnership Forms — Federal

U.S. Partnership Return of Income   1065

Application for Automatic Extension of Time to File a Return
    for a U.S. Partnership or for Certain Trusts   8736

Partners' Shares of Income, Credits, Deductions, etc.
    Schedule K (1065)

Corporation Forms — Federal

U.S. Corporation Income Tax Return   1120

Alternative Minimum Tax — Corporations   4626

Application for Automatic Extension of Time to file
    Corporation Income Tax Return   7004

S Corporation Forms — Federal

U.S. Income Tax Return for an S Corporation   1120S

Shareholder's Share of Income, Credits, Deductions, etc.
    Schedule K-1 (1120S)

Order Form

Business Books are our Business!

■ **The Loan Book: Complete Step by Step Guide to Getting a Business or Personal Loan**
by Orlando J. Antonini and Casey C. Colley
_____Copies $19.95 paperback
Written and designed to meet the needs of people seeking loans. After an overview of
the loan process, the authors show you how to prepare the necessary financial statements,
both for business and personal loans.

■ **Business Persons' Guide to Taxation in the 90's: Starting and Running Your Business**
by Harry Gordon Oliver
_____Copies $19.95 paperback
Covers all states and answers all your business tax questions.
"A useful guide for small-business owners overwhelmed by the paperwork assosciated
with running a company..."   —Los Angeles Times

■ **How to Avoid the Hidden Costs of Doing Business in California**
by Harry Gordon Oliver
_____Copies $19.95 paperback
_____Copies $35.00 3-ring binder
"Concise and comprehensive, Gordon Oliver's publication is one-stop business consulting
at a minimal cost."   —Edwin A. Okamura, Executive Director, Asian Business League

Amount enclosed: $_____ (plus $2.00 postage and handling)
Order two books or more books and the postage and handling are on us.
(California residents add 6.75% sales tax.)

_____
Name
_____
Organization
_____
Address
_____
City   State   Zip

Send to: El Dorado Press P.O. Box 1755 Lafayette, CA 94549
          Phone (415) 932-1383 Fax (415) 934-8277